Focused Wealth

A Canadian's

Common Sense Guide

to Financial Prosperity

Jeffery A Keill

CFP CIM FMA

Copyright © 2016 Jeffery A Keill

All rights reserved.

The author has asserted his moral right to be identified as the author of this work.

All rights reserved. No part of this publication may be reproduced, stored in a retrieval system, or transmitted in any form or by any means—electronic, mechanical, photocopying, recording, or otherwise—without prior permission from the author or publisher.

NOTE: The content of this book is for information and educational purposes only, and it is not meant to replace professional advice from an experienced financial planner. Please exercise due diligence and conduct thorough research before investing with any adviser. Opinions expressed are those of the author.

Published by:
Perissos Media
www.PerissosMedia.com

ISBN-13: 978-1539657750

To contact Mr Keill for professional advice or media information, you may use the details below:

Phone (Ontario, Canada): 613-253-8934 **Int'l:** +1-613-253-8934

Fill out an online request here: www.JeffKeill.com

CONTENTS

Testimonials v

Acknowledgements vii

Foreword ix

Introduction 1

Chapter 1 ~ Tempus Fugit 3

    Frank's Story 3

    Life is about choices. Choose wisely. 8

Chapter 2 ~ You are going to die! 11

    Barney's story 11

    Life is finite! 13

    Personal Financial Lifecycle 16

    You are a mini-corporation 18

Chapter 3 ~ The Reality of Financial Security Today 23

    Hugh's Story 23

    The New Retirement Reality 25

Chapter 4 ~ Focused Financial Security 33

    Trinity's story 33

    Defining Financial Freedom 38

Chapter 5 ~ Saving, Investing and Speculation 47
    Jak's Story 47
    Saving Versus Investing 57
    Investing vs Speculation 59

Chapter 6 ~ Capital Market History: Owners vs Loaners 63
    Sarah's Story 63
    What is a capital market? 68
    Ownership vs Loanership 70
    Capital Market History 71
    What is risk? 73
    What is the rate of return? 77
    Is there relationship between risk and return? 78

Chapter 7 ~ The Intellectual Framework 81
    Alexander's Story 81
    The Noise 88
    Personal Wealth Management Strategy 92
    Investment Policy Statement 95

Chapter 8 ~ The Asset Allocation Method 101
    Jakob Fuggar's Story 101
    Diversification 107

How to Diversify 110

Strategic Asset Allocation 112

Dynamic Asset Allocation 116

Chapter 9 ~ Price and Value 119

Dee and Sharon's Story 119

Intrinsic Value 129

Crack Cocaine and Party on the Stock Market 134

Chapter 10 ~ Botulism, Salmonella and E. Coli 139

Mitch and Meg's Story 139

Hamburger Logic 143

Results or Price ? 147

Do you need a Financial Advisor or Wealth Manager? 151

Choosing your Wealth Advisor 152

Summary 159

YOUR Story 159

Your Next Step 167

About the Author 169

About the Publisher 170

TESTIMONIALS

"*Focused Wealth* is a must read for anyone who wants proven inside secrets to achieving financial freedom and peace of mind."

Carol Ring, CPA
CEO, The Culture Connection

"In this era of information overload, it is nice to read a book which simplifies the concepts of financial security and keeps it interesting with pertinent stories. Jeff makes investing intelligible, just as he has done for us over the last twenty years."

Sharon Holzscherer, Author
Patterns of Disorder

"A captivating read. Jeff is able to take a difficult subject and make it humorous and readable. He makes you look at your financial plan with a new perspective."

Elizabeth Swarbrick, LLB
Lawyer, Mediator

"Read this book! Jeff shares a simple yet strategic money mindset that will benefit you for years to come."

Michael J. Hughes
North America's Networking Guru

"This book contains simple ideas from a well-seasoned advisor, ideas which investors can apply immediately to order to increase their financial wealth."

Rahim Dhalla
Director, Portfolio Management, Counsel Portfolio Services

"The ability to convey a complex topic in a simplistic manner is an art. Once again, Jeff has succeeded in imparting his diverse knowledge of an ever-increasingly technical financial landscape with this book."

Hunter Graves, J.D.
Lawyer

ACKNOWLEDGEMENTS

As with all projects in life, nothing is possible on our own. This book is no exception. If it wasn't for the support and input of so many people, this venture would have ended before it began.

All of the content comes from experiences that I have had with people of far greater wisdom than myself. I am truly richer for their sharing, and I hope that this book is a continuation of that human condition of individual sharing for the benefit of all.

Thank you in particular to the late Sarah McKay with whom I have spent many years working and who was taken far too soon from this earth. I truly wish that she could have been here to read and critique this book.

Thank you also to my colleagues and business associates, present and past, who challenged my thinking everyday: Sherrye Emery, Anik Levesque, Meaghan Buttemer, Susan Cole, Paul Scully, David McGruer, Omari Whyte, David Bartley, Sam Febbraro and Chris Reynolds.

Thank you to my publisher, Jerry Kuzma from PerissosMedia.com, for his patience and his ability to keep me on task.

To my family, I extend a thank you as well, for you have given me lots of material to work with over the years; to my parents for their support; to my sister Cathy who inspires me, even when she is on the other side of the country; to my children, Alex and Beth, for whom I am truly blessed to have in my life. You give life more meaning and purpose.

Thank you to my wife Teresa, who with unfailing charm and dedication has been through this journey by my side for over 25 years. She is my biggest cheerleader.

I would also like to thank all of my clients, past and present, for their trust and confidence. I might work hard to help you achieve your financial goals, but you have given back to me much more than you could ever imagine. I cherish our relationship, and I look forward to a continued mutually-prosperous future together.

Finally, I would like to thank the Big Guy upstairs. Without Him, none of this would have been possible.

~ Jeff Keill
September 1st, 2016

FOREWORD

As a lifelong student of the global financial industry, I have been exposed to hundreds of financial planning books and thousands of articles over my career. These publications have ranged from sophisticated, technical analysis that is designed purely for academics at one extreme to simple tips and illustrations written for the lay person at the other extreme. In most cases, it is rare to satisfy and indulge both academics and lay people in one body of work.

Jeff has succeeded to challenge both ends of the spectrum and everyone in between. Starting each chapter with short stories, the book offers a delightful yet compelling narrative of examples and analogies; one cannot help but think that the main character in the story is you or someone you know. More specifically, these stories provide an innocent escape for the reader in order to appreciate the life lesson in each chapter.

This is then followed by historical facts, definitions and exercises to educate the novice investor, while it reminds the experienced reader of the principles that they may have taken for granted or perhaps forgotten over the years.

Thereafter, Jeff provides a comprehensive prescription for all Canadians, regardless of age, gender, financial knowledge, risk tolerance or time horizon, in order to reach their financial goals and objectives. The last section provides a convenient and useful summary of the seven concepts outlined in the book. More importantly, a list of important action items follows each concept, acting like an invaluable checklist of "common sense" for future reference and accountability.

Vincent Van Gogh once said, *"Great things are done by a series of small things brought together."* Folks, there is no silver bullet or a secret trick of the trade to expedite or guarantee financial prosperity. It is, in fact, a series of many small, medium and large actions throughout our lives that help us to pursue and ultimately achieve our financial goals and objectives.

Working with a trusted wealth advisor is just one of those actions to get us started, keep us accountable during our financial adventure and guide us through our journey of life. Now that is just common sense. Enjoy!

Sam Febbraro
President & CEO of Counsel Portfolio Services Inc
EVP of Investment Planning Counsel Inc

INTRODUCTION

When I first started as a wealth advisor in 1991, the financial landscape was already becoming complex and daunting for the average investor. There was uncertainty in the markets, the economy was about to unravel after a recession, the geopolitical landscape in Europe was a mess, the Middle East was in chaos and the United States debt was soaring.

Has anything really changed 25 years later?

Has it become harder to achieve our individual financial goals? Our debt levels are higher, children are staying at home longer, retirement seems so far away and taxes continue to eat into our income daily.

On the surface, so much has changed. Deep down, however, I want to share with you the news that you can take courage. The good news for you is that the basic truths about wealth and money have not changed.

It is quite obvious that there are significant changes or shifts in technology, health care and culture. We have seen the demise of some old industries and the rising of some new ones: mail vs email, cable vs satellite, telephones vs video conferencing, buying a CD versus downloading, and the list goes on.

These changes cannot be denied, but many things remain the same, though they are wrapped in different clothing. We still wage wars but on different enemies. We still entrust our countries but to different leaders. We still listen to music, though in a different format. We are still connected to world issues, though not by newspapers.

Even in the world of personal finance, we have witnessed the fall of interest rates, only to see the rise of alternative investments. The wealth management waters that most investors need to wade through have become shark-infested, with warning signs that are written in a different language. Our simple terms from just a few decades ago have become littered with acronyms and jargon. All of this creates a perfect storm for many people to simply do nothing (which, in itself, is doing something).

Truly, we still go through our day in the same way. We wake up, work during the day, come home to family and go to bed. In between all of this, we still eat, clothe ourselves, seek friendship, enjoy being in love, cherish our family and try to fend off our inevitable death.

Regardless of all the superficial changes, even our financial goals have not changed: we all want to reduce our debt, pay less taxes, own a home, educate our children and retire in comfort. We are still wired to weigh up risk versus reward. Many of us still make decisions based on fear and greed.

This book is intended to bring back the common sense and fundamental truths about money, investing and financial freedom. When the financial world wants to talk about the last 20 minutes, I want to talk about the truths learned over the last 200 years. That is why I start most of the chapters with short stories about real people and the financial lessons that they have learned—the same principles that you and I need to follow in our financial lives in the present.

I want you to know that reaching your financial goals in a world that has become overly complex can still be accomplished. This can be done quite easily when you get the right people to help you.

I wrote this book for YOU. I want to help you to achieve your financial goals. I want to show you the tools that keep simplicity at the core of the decision making process, so that you can stay *focused on your wealth*.

CHAPTER 1 ~ TEMPUS FUGIT

Tempus fugit when you're having fun!

The Latin phrase *"tempus fugit"* is translated as *"time flies"*. It is not a new concept, but it is one that is getting much more attention these days. This next illustration shows us the speed at which time can fly past us as well as the results of being caught out by the passing of time.

Frank's story

The sun was bright and warm as it shone directly on Frank's face. This was the first morning that he was able to stretch out his legs and really take a wander around the neighbourhood.

A sharp pang in the depths of his empty belly reminded him that eating would be the first item on his to-do list. Along the way, Frank met a few other caterpillars who were out for their first walk among the branches of the grand oak tree.

None of the other caterpillars were as beautiful as he was. Frank was a brilliant combination of yellow and orange with four neon green spots displayed on his back. He was not like most of the others, who were a more common shade of light brown and were complimented by a white stripe.

The other caterpillars had found succulent leaves and were enjoying their feast. Nibbling happily, they were filling their bellies in the big oak that they called home. Frank, the brilliant little orange and green spotted caterpillar, was not going to settle for just any leaf. He wanted the biggest and juiciest leaf on the whole oak tree. "The day is so long," Frank thought to himself, "that there is plenty of time and there are plenty of leaves to choose from."

As the little orange and green caterpillar made his way along the branch, he passed many leaves of different sizes, many of a desirable dark green colour. Frank would stop and analyse each opportunity, but the next one just a little further along seemed even bigger and tastier. Leaf after leaf, branch after branch, Frank continued to search for the most perfect leaf as the sun moved across the blue sky. There was always something about each leaf that was not exactly what he wanted.

The sun was now getting closer to the crest of the horizon and it was preparing for its own nightly slumber. Most of the other caterpillars on the branch were taking the final hours to relax in the sun while their food digested. In the meantime, Frank was still looking for the perfect leaf.

He checked out each one until he finally got to the last leaf on the branch. It wasn't any better or any worse than the other leaves he had found all day. This particular leaf was going to have to do. Frank was tired and weak. He felt that the day had passed him by, and it seemed that not eating had caused his brilliant colours to fade.

The next morning, Frank awoke to a second beautiful day in the oak tree. The sun was as bright and warm as the day before. It was a perfect day to relax on the branch and nibble on the remainder of the leaf from the day before. The little orange and green caterpillar nibbled away and then fell asleep in the hot sun.

When the sun was almost at its highest in the sky, Frank woke to the noise of busy caterpillars preparing their cocoons. "Why rush?" he wondered. "Such a beautiful day should be enjoyed." It was still early and he was sure that there was plenty of time.

Frank thought that a brilliant and wonderful caterpillar as he was should have the best cocoon ever. As the other caterpillars began to cocoon, Frank sat and watched. The day was so long and there was plenty of time. He watched and analysed each of their cocoons as they began to build.

Frank then set off to examine all the tiny branches on which his majestic cocoon would hang. Just like the leaf, he found not a single branch that was better or worse than any other. He continued his search as the sun passed its highest point in the sky. Frank strolled along branch by branch in the grand oak tree, watching all his caterpillar neighbours finishing their cocoons. None of them would be as good as his when he was ready to start.

The sun was low on the horizon when Frank realized that he had not started his cocoon. Somehow the sun had seemed to sneak across the sky without warning. The time was quickly running out and so he frantically took a nearby branch and hastily began to cocoon himself. The branch was weak and barely supported the caterpillar. It was now dark, and Frank, with his faded coat, frantically worked to finish his pod. Frank realized that his cocoon would not be ready in time.

Frank, the once brilliant orange and green caterpillar, would not become a brilliant and colourful butterfly with everyone else. How fast time flies.

The world today is as dynamic and wonderful as it ever has been. More than ever, Canadians now have the ability to see the world in so many new and exciting ways. We have more wealth as our economy matures. We have more time as we are living longer. We have more ability to see the world as travel becomes simpler.

We even have easier access to information. At any time and in almost any location, we can simply visit far-away lands, learn how to create something or keep in touch with friends via the internet while having a morning coffee or commuting to work.

So, with all of these wonderful things being so abundant in our lives, why do some people miss the boat when it comes to planning their financial lives? Why do some people seem to prosper financially while others simply get left behind? Why, in a world that is brimming with ample opportunity, do some find they are not able to achieve any success at obtaining wealth?

Sit there for a moment and think to yourself about how time seems to whiz by. Twenty years ago seems like twenty minutes ago. Time rages past, and the older we get, the faster time seems to fly by us.

As we get older, the amount of time we have left becomes shorter. The older we get, the faster each passing year seems to occur. Instead of anxiously waiting for Christmas as a child, we find it sneaking up on us faster each year. It seems as though Christmas not only sneaks up but it also blows right past, and before you know it, you are planning for Easter and then suddenly it is Christmas once again.

I frequently hear people talk about how the years have passed. They say that it seems like only yesterday that they had gotten married, graduated school, had children or retired. Most of the time, it is followed with comments such as, "If I only knew then what I know now." How many times have you said the same thing?

So why is this happening? Here are three notable theories that are held by psychologists to help us understand this phenomenon.

First-time events become less frequent. Things like our first date, first kiss, first day at high school and first day driving no longer occur in the present. Days seem to be filled with re-occurring events. Although new experiences do still occur, they are far less frequent.

For example, imagine that you travel to an all-inclusive resort in Cuba. The new experiences are happening every moment when you first get there. Your first day or so seems to pass slowly. The thought of having a whole week seems like plenty of time. After you have accustomed yourself to the location, routine, the food and the experience, the week passes fairly quickly. Before you know it, you are back on the flight home. Extend this same concept out over your life and it can have the same effect.

Time's passage is relative to age. We are constantly comparing time periods with the experiences that we have already lived through. For example, one year to a 5-year-old is 20% of his life. One year to a 50-year-old is 2% of their life. There is a significant difference that I notice when I am working with a young family in their twenties as compared to an older couple in their seventies.

If I am discussing "long term" with them, the definition has different meanings for each. To the 25-year-old person, the "long term" generally means approximately 10 to 20 years. To a 75-year-old person, the term greatly equates to 25 or 30 years. Of course, this is a general statement but it is one that has proven true more often than not.

As we age, we pay less attention to time. When you are a child, you begin counting each day coming up to Christmas as soon as the Nativity calendar starts on December 1st. As an adult, your focus is more on mundane and day-to-day needs, such as paying bills, going to work and preparing meals. Ask the busy parents of two active children how often they get to sit down and have a meaningful talk about planning something.

Outside of the notable milestone birthdays (which make us feel older), most people look at birthdays as "just another birthday". The same happens with other events, such as anniversaries, work and marriage. Your first year at work is notable, while your 17th year is not even worth mentioning. The 26th year of marriage is a passing accomplishment but the 25th year was something to celebrate.

Life is about choices. Choose wisely.

A famous hamburger chain in Canada tells consumers to "have it your way". Another famous sandwich chain allows you to order any submarine sandwich you want, as it is available on nine different breads with over 30 toppings to choose from. This is not only limited to the restaurant industry. If you wanted to plan a trip, build a house, buy tires, choose a cellphone plan, order a cable service or even buy groceries, you have hundreds (even thousands) of options to choose from.

One of the most popular mustard brands in Canada is now offering over 10 different flavours of mustard. Imagine that you can fill your fridge door with different flavours of mustard along with your traditional plain yellow version. That is just one condiment! Imagine how many condiments you could have when you combine the same concept with other basic toppings like mayonnaise, ketchup, relish, hot sauces, and pickles. Do yourself a favour the next time you open your refrigerator door: count the number of condiments and toppings you have available for use. Next, ask yourself how often you use them and if you actually need them.

Henry Ford is credited with saying (although there is no proof he actually said it) that, "They can have their car painted any colour they like, as long as it is black." This sounds like a crazy statement in today's world of custom designs and personalization.

Today's world is all about choice: choice of color, choice of flavour, choice of material and choice of add-ons. Choice-choice-choice. Choose–choose-choose. Life is a series of never-ending choices. Some of these are simple or involuntary, like getting up in the morning or going to bed. Some are more complex, like marriage, children or retirement.

Either way, we all have to choose many things each and every day. Some of the choices have little or no impact on our long term success. Some others can be life-altering. We all know that we need to tread carefully and make wise choices. It is really difficult to tell the important decisions from the less important ones when you are pelted with options.

With all these choices to make in our lives, the world we live in provides us with all the information we need to make the choices. We can get immediate answers to anything; they can end up being right or wrong, but they are answers nonetheless.

An "eponymous verb" is used to describe an action which is derived from a person or thing it was named after. In today's world of access to information, one of the most recently developed eponymous verbs is "google". If you were asked to "google" something, you would most likely know exactly what you are being asked. If someone said they "googled" the answer, you would know what they meant. You would probably even say you googled it if you used some other search engine instead of Google.

The point is that information and the ability to get it are commodities with very low cost and high ease of accessibility. As a growing teenager, you were probably told to get off your backside and open a dictionary to find a definition. You learned that you needed to go to the library to read about certain topics. This is not something that many of us would do today.

Many people would argue that the more choices we have, the better we are. Many people would also argue that the more information we have, the better we are able to make those wise choices. The question is not whether choice or information is a good thing; rather, what quantity of choice or information is too much. At what point does too much choice and information become debilitating to the person trying to choose something? Can information overload lead to a stalemate, where the only choice being made is not to choose?

When I first started working as a financial planner, someone taught me the term we use to describe this problem. This term is "analysis paralysis", and it results when an investor is given too many facts, many of which contradict each other.

This overload of facts ultimately leads to the investor becoming stunned, like a deer in the headlights of an oncoming car, totally unable to make a decision. Lengths of time would be spent trying to make a decision, whether hours, days, weeks or even months. No decision is ever made because the options and information are overwhelming. This non-decision becomes the unintended decision, bringing with it unexpected consequences.

Over the years of working with individuals and families, I see that the same problem occurs in many facets of life. Not only has picking the right mustard become daunting, people find that they have a hard time picking the best investment option, the best financial strategy, the best mortgage, the best time to retire or the best of anything. There are too many choices with too much information available.

When you combine the effects of "analysis paralysis" and "tempus fugit", you create the perfect storm that blows against the financial success of many people. This is why some people's choice is to not choose, and before they know it, time has passed them by.

In the next few chapters, I want to explain how you can take back control of your financial life and how to apply basic truths about money, investing and financial security. Using a common sense approach with time-tested concepts, I want to help you cut through the information clutter and make simple yet precise choices in your financial life.

CHAPTER 2 ~ YOU ARE GOING TO DIE!

Life is finite! You are going to die. As strange as it sounds, the sooner you appreciate this, the quicker we can begin the process of planning for your financial success. If you are one of those extremely rare cases who will live on earth forever, I encourage you to pass this book on to a friend or return it to me for a full refund. However, if you think that you will one day pass away like all of the great men before you, then this book is for you!

Barney's story

Sleep had changed for Barney lately. No longer was he able to enjoy sleeping in, even past the time when most people would have risen and started their journey to work.

After retirement, he relished staying in bed and drifting in and out of sleep, recalling how he used to catch the morning commuter bus. On this early Thursday morning, Barney once again found himself unable to sleep any longer. Yet another day, well before the sun had risen, he tossed and turned in his king-size bed. He stared into the dark air that hovered above him. It wasn't the empty space beside him where his wife had slept that caused him to stir lately.

Even after five years had passed, the pain from her passing was still fresh, but this was a physical inability to sleep. Even the light rain dancing on the tin roof of his little shed outside his window and the cool moist spring breeze coming in the room couldn't keep him. He found that stringing together more than six hours of sleep became a chore, no matter how much he enjoyed just lying in bed.

Barney pulled himself out of bed slowly but with intent, which included his famous wide-armed stretch. He thought he looked like a great eagle spreading its wings, remembering the bald eagle he saw many years ago during a west coast trip. Perched like royalty on top of a hydro pole with its majestic grey wings and its white crown, it declared once again its dominance as king of the sky. This was Barney each morning, except that his crown was formed from a lack of hair now.

After throwing on his plaid robe and slippers, he made his way carefully down the flight of stairs to the main floor and into the kitchen. The life-long habit of having a coffee brewing before anything else was alive and well, even if there was no need for the effects of caffeine anymore. The coffee habit had started well before spending thirty-five years as a civil servant. His wife was never the coffee drinker, but she was always the one to make the first pot each morning. Four cups a day was the standard: one cup when he woke, one cup for the half-hour commute and two cups at work while at his desk.

This morning coffee routine was not so much a conscious action as it was an automatic response to getting out of bed. So was the mug he used every morning for the past 15 years. Barney went into the music room where he liked to sit and read. He left the favourite mug on the little table beside his favourite reading chair, a red leather wingback chair that could recline if you knew about the secret feature. The centrepiece of the room was a large fireplace that was guarded on each side by impressive bookshelves containing his favourite books, curiosities and family photo albums. It was one photo album in particular that caught his attention as he reached for his mug.

The photo album was a blood red colour with gold edging Barney sat on the edge of his red leather wingback chair and leafed through the photos. The images were of Barney when he was leaving home to attend university in the city. Inside he chuckled at how thin his size was and how thick his hair. He remembered fondly the brown jacket he was wearing—the same jacket that he threw around his future wife's shoulders after their first date.

The pages he looked at turned from days to years and album after album. Barney sat in wonder about how much foresight his wife had in compiling all their years together. She was always the thoughtful servant and planner.

Under his breath he thanked her, and out loud he shared a few moments of laughter and deep sorrow with her as if she was present. To him, she was there. To him, she sat beside him on the chair, even at times on his lap snuggled closely against his plaid robe. Over the next two hours, he turned one page after the next. Barney realized that as the black and white pictures slowly changed to colour, his slim waist size grew, his dark hair turned to white and the memories become even more vibrant.

These albums contained a picture journey of his life, through the years of learning, working and retiring. The journey on those pages included pictures of their first car, their first house, travels to faraway places, their kids and grandchildren and their retirement years. The last book was the hardest to get through, as it was the final years before his wife passed. At the end of the album there were only five pages left--five blank pages yet to be filled.

Barney, on the red leather wingback chair, laid the last album open to the blank pages. He grabbed his mug and went to the kitchen to get his first cup of coffee. His day had changed and the sun hadn't even risen.

Life is finite!

Why would I start a chapter with such a sad story? Why be so morbid in a book in which I want to give hope and a promise of a better financial life? Am I trying to be a *shock-jockey* to wake you up? Well, quite frankly, YES!

Wake up! You are going to die.

Financial planning is based on the same basic foundation as economics. We want to discover how to allocate a limited amount of resources to achieve the optimal result towards a desired goal. In other words, we have only so much of some resources in order to accomplish all that we want. The most important of all the resources we have available is time. Time itself is more valuable than anything and it is this precious commodity that we must learn how to allocate.

To stress this point, let me walk you through a simple exercise that I use as a finance professor at the local college. We will assume that you will live to be 80-years-old. It brings home the point of our mortality and it quantifies the resource of time.

Start by grabbing a piece of paper, a napkin or anything that you can write on. Now write down your **date of birth**. Do not write just the year but the whole date. For example, let's say that you were born on April 10, 1960. Once you have done this, the next step is using simple math. Add 80 to the year of your birth. In our example, you would arrive at an answer of 2040. Now attach the day and month of your birth and you arrive at the day that you will reach the last of your 80 years.

For the sake of discussion only, we will declare this your **date of demise.** Of course, it goes without saying that many people live longer than 80 years of age, and many die much sooner than that. Further to this, life expectancy is also based on other things like your sex, your smoking habit, family history and other factors.

Now, on a piece of paper, draw a line about six inches long. At the far left point of the line, write your date of birth. At the far right end of the line, write your *date of demise*. This will graphically depict your life from beginning to end.

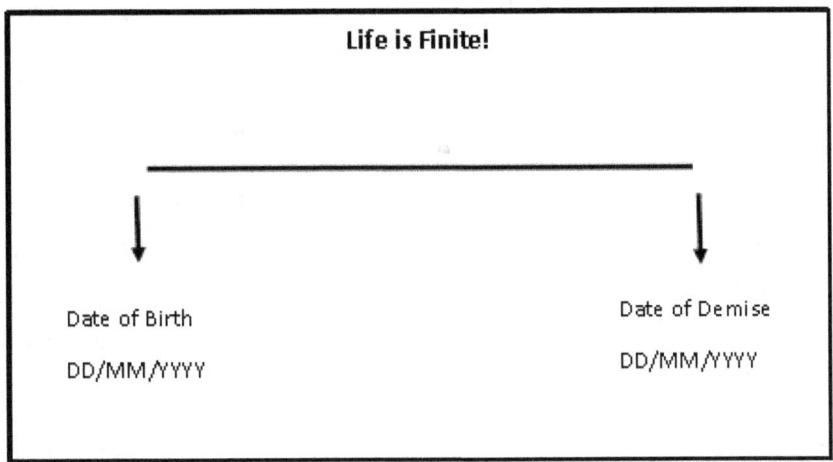

The purpose of this exercise is not to predict or predetermine when you are going to die, but it is merely to put into perspective how long you have on God's green acre. We are born and we will die. As we get older and time continues to pass, we are continuing to walk down a shortening path.

As we would plan how to spend our limited money, we should consider how we intend to spend our limited time. As we would budget our finances, we could also budget our life. We would segment our financial budget based on basic necessities, leisure and savings. We can also segment our time by work, play and family time. Of course, one of the main reasons for writing this book in the first place is this: people tend to do neither of these basic tasks and yet wonder why they don't succeed.

Why is this the case? **It is because of procrastination.**

One of the biggest demons that individuals have to contend with is their own procrastination devil. Upon one of our shoulders sits the little white devil, telling us to get off the couch, while on the other shoulder sits the little red devil, telling us to ignore the other shoulder because we can always do it later. We all know that, deep down, we *should* flick the red one off and listen to the white one. However, the red one seems to speak louder and more convincingly.

Procrastination erodes time. As inflation erodes the purchasing power of money, procrastination therefore chews away at the most important commodity we have in achieving our goals. Each day that passes without taking advantage of it is one more day that we will never get back.

Procrastination, from a financial planning point of view, stems from what I believe to be five main reasons:

- I don't know how: How do I start when I don't know where to start?
- Fear of failure: What if I try and I fail?
- Fear of success: What if I try and succeed? Then what?
- It is boring: Why should I do this when I can do something much more pleasurable?
- You can't make me: the rebellious refusal.

There may only be one reason in your life, but, most of the time, it is a combination of a few different reasons. Regardless of the reason for our own procrastination, all of us must defeat this demon each and every day. As we progress through the book, we will look a little closer at each of these concerns and how to address them.

Personal Financial Lifecycle

With your life being finite and death being certain, the irony is that it makes financial planning (and therefore life planning) so much easier and predictable. I guess that I am trying to say that you can take comfort that you will not live forever!

Imagine trying to plan out a life that did not have defined periods beautifully laid out as we have. Imagine a life that had no end. How would immortals ever plan to spend their days, weeks or years if they were not to die? Planning would be a wasted venture as there would be no need to do it.

Here is a strange contrast to our consistent fight for longevity. I am sure that if every person walking the face of the earth was to live forever, we would be fighting to find a cure for immortality. We are a funny group of creatures.

Of course, we do not live forever, as we already talked about. We will have a date of birth and a date of demise. The former we know about and the latter is yet to come, but it shall surely come. Ask yourself if there are other key periods that can help to divide up our lifespan and life plan. The answer is yes.

Students who have taken any basic business courses will know that a business has three distinct phases in its life[i]. It begins, it grows and it matures. This is called the business lifecycle, and there are certain characteristics in each of the three phases.

The beginning is called the *start-up phase,* which generally consists of low revenue, high costs and little market share. Sales are low and product costs are high, as the business is still being developed. The second phase is called the *growth phase,* and it generally has rising sales revenue, lowering costs and increasing market share. The third phase is known as the *maturity phase.* This phase consists of stable sales revenue, low consistent costs and stronger market share.

In personal finance, we have the same distinct phases. The names of the three phases might be different, but the characteristics are very much alike. The three phases are: Learn, Earn and Yearn.

You are a mini-corporation

To completely understand the stages, you have to first appreciate that we are all individual businesses. Each one of us is a *personal services corporation* that chooses, at some point, to hire out our services to either an employer or customers (if you are self-employed).

Our personal services corporation will demand revenue from the marketplace which is dependent on the supply and demand of our particular service offering. More specialized skills demand higher revenue in return. More general or simple skill sets that many people offer could not justify the same high revenue.

For example, compare a heart surgeon to a clerk at a local retail store. You would never allow the clerk at the local shoe store to perform open heart surgery on you. It might be smart to heed their advice when it comes to choosing your next pair of loafers, but you would not want him to perform an angioplasty or coronary artery bypass grafting. One might ease your sole, but the other could save your life!

Your personal services corporation has all the basic departments and hierarchy of a company. A business has various common departments, such as research and development, human resources, manufacturing, marketing, sales and, of course, finance. Depending on the time of day, you wear much the same hats when you get a diploma or degree (research and development), apply for a job (marketing/sales), work hard to keep your job (manufacturing) and watch the income and expenses (finance). All through your life, these departments will become more or less important as time goes on.

If we take this analogy one step further, we can introduce the concept of other stakeholders once an individual is married or has children. The spouse and children then form a special relationship with the personal services corporation as the individual moves into a kind of chief executive role. The addition of these people to an individual is akin to shareholders becoming connected to a family company. They are dependent on the success of the personal services corporation for their own success.

The first phase of the personal financial lifecycle entails learning about life and developing as a person, and that is why I call it the "learn phase". For the first 25 years of life, we spend much of our time learning about the world around us. First, we learn about our own immediate needs, and then we learn about the needs of our immediate family.

We then turn our focus to people at school and to society in general. We learn simple things such as human interaction, reading, writing and the human experience. Once we leave elementary school, we begin to learn more academically about the world with practical science, social sciences, history, geography and similar topics.

When we finish high school, we have, for the most part, a strong inclination of what we "want to be when we grow up". This is the starting point where we begin our specialization for the personal services corporation that we want to run. We make a conscious effort to attend post-secondary school of some sort in order to better refine the skills we want to bring to the marketplace.

This is one of the first big choices that we have to make in life: "What do you want to be when you grow up?" When you were 10-years-old, you could easily dream and say what you wanted to do, but it is around age 18 when you begin to feel the need to make a decision and choose a career for yourself.

Of course, you have a choice, as we always have choices to make. You could choose to do nothing; however, doing nothing is an act of your volition and it slows down your corporate growth.

When we attend post-secondary school, it is often because we were guided by parents or teachers to do this. You, or someone in your life, realized the importance of building your skills through education. It is the same as a business doing research and development on a product to make it better so that it can demand a superior price in the marketplace.

The first phase, the *learning phase*, is really about building market value for our own personal service offering. In this phase, just like in the first phase of the business cycle, it is drenched with debt and it is dry of any meaningful income. Student loans and summer job wages are very much like a new business burning through capital to bring an idea from concept to prototype to finished product. Once the product is developed, it gets released into the world. In the second phase, we start to grow. We have now left behind the formal full-time school days and moved into an employment. The second phase is called the *earning phase*. We have built our basic product and honed our initial service offering for our personal services corporation. Now it is about slowly gaining traction and thereafter increasing market share.

A business in the second phase, the *growth phase*, has its product to market and is starting to sell more and more of it. The more of its product that it sells, the more revenue it has to pay down debt and start to pay dividends to its shareholders. As we further develop, our personal services corporation continues to grow from its experiences. We refine ourselves into a better offering in the marketplace with both knowledge and experience.

The individual in the second phase of the personal financial lifecycle begins to move up the ladder and to attain higher earnings. As earnings increase, the amount of debt starts to get paid down at a faster and faster rate. Whereas our late 20's and early 30's were marked by relatively low earnings, we start to experience some of our highest earning years by our late 50's. Sometimes the earnings are two or three times what we earned when we first started working, which makes sense as the value of our personal services corporation has also increased.

When we finished formal schooling, we gained knowledge. By the time we get to the latter part of the *earn phase,* we have gained experience. There is a saying that, in my opinion, is just plain wrong: "Knowledge is Power". I disagree with this, as it is one thing to read about a screwdriver, but it is another to know how to turn it. Knowledge is nothing without experience. You can have a lot of knowledge, but the true value of knowledge is knowing where and when to use it. This is why experience is so important and can be rewarded so handsomely.

The final phase in the personal financial lifecycle is the *yearning phase.* I know the term seems a little strange, but it really was the best one that rhymed with the first two! The *yearning phase* is simply the phase in our lives where our long-term financial viability has been achieved and can be maintained with great certainty. The individual begins to yearn for less time at work with a sustained predictable income, so that more time can be spent experiencing various personal adventures.

In the business lifecycle, this is known as the *maturity phase*. In the *maturity phase,* a business experiences consistent levels of income with predictable and manageable levels of debt. The product that the business first brought to market many years ago continues to enjoy sustained revenue in excess of costs.

For your personal services corporation, the time and effort you put into building your brand has created a steady flow of income. This has allowed you to build a pool of capital that can provide for your retirement. To put it simply, you educated yourself, you got a good job, you enjoyed an excellent level of income and you saved enough to live comfortably for the remainder of your life.

We will all experience life. Granted, some will live longer and some shorter, but we all get a chance from the day we are born. In our finite life, we will see many things as Barney did in the story at the start of this chapter. Our lives, our "one kick at the can", can pass by us without notice. We can measure its length with some degree of precision and layout general periods or phases.

We each have our own photo albums, containing 20 pages with 10 photo slots yet to be filled. As we enter each picture, be it of school, work, family or retirement, the pages and albums are getting filled.

The first step in financial planning is to know the available resources we have and how they will be used to maximize their value in our life. What pictures do you want in your album?

---

i. In some business books, there may be a fourth phase, known as the Decline Phase. I have not included it here for the same reason that there is no 13th floor in a building and there is no Chapter 11 in this book. We don't need to waste space with negative thinking

CHAPTER 3 ~ THE REALITY OF FINANCIAL SECURITY TODAY

Hugh's story

It was cold and windy, typical of an early Canadian January morning in the countryside of Tyotown Glen. The snow, although not overly deep, provided enough of a white blanket to erase any evidence of a green lawn that existed only a month ago.

Hugh peered out from the glass patio door into the yard which backed onto snow-covered fields. The hay fields rolled over a hill that made the horizon seem a little closer, and it provided a line between the white snow and the blue sky above it. In front of him, the wind wisped up the fresh top layer of snow and was twirling around like a classical ballerina wearing a snow white gown. Today was Hugh's 80th birthday.

His wife was busy setting up tables for the expectant family who would arrive soon enough. Children, grandchildren and a small scattering of great-grandchildren would all pour loudly through the door in a few hours. None of his lifelong friends could be there, as more than half of them had passed away or were not able to easily travel anymore. Hugh had been to more than his share of funerals in the last ten years.

Pretending not to hear the calls to help set up more card tables, Hugh silently watched his snow ballerina rise and fall as she continued to pirouette and glide across the snowy floor.

Hugh thought back over his eighty years of life. He could remember being a young child, watching the same performance from the window of his bedroom on the family farm.

THE REALITY OF FINANCIAL SECURITY TODAY

Over eighty years, the same dancer would show up in the winter months just to dazzle him with her skill and finesse. It was a relationship that existed only for mere minutes each winter, but it was clearly etched in his memory. Those eighty years were a mix of hardship, prosperity, adventure, love, happiness and tragedy.

Hugh was born into a typically large Catholic family. There was not much money to go around, so as soon as Hugh was old enough, it became important for him to help earn money for himself and his family. He wasn't very good at many subjects in school, but he loved to work with his hands and to build things. Going to high school was possible, but the lack of money and the requirements at home stopped him from heading to college. Grade eight would be the last time Hugh sat at a desk in a school.

There were many cold winters during his years. Many men found it difficult to obtain well-paid labour, leaving the family farms to find industrial work in the cities. Just prior to leaving for WWII Europe, Hugh met and married his first wife, Verna. The next several decades of his life were spent providing for their family. After gaining a reputation for hard work and fairness, Hugh established his own construction business. The years that followed were full of hardship and then followed by a growing prosperity. Life was pretty good in those middle years. Earnings were good and they saved what they could so that life could continue during their retirement.

Tragedy struck, as it so often does, when they least expected it. By her early 50's, Verna was diagnosed with cancer. The next several years were just as prosperous financially, but the ability to enjoy them became less and less. Verna passed away a few years later. Even as Hugh looked out the window, the thought of Verna's death still sat heavy in his heart, and it was a painful page in Hugh's life.

A few years later, Hugh did remarry, and the couple was now

preparing for his 80th birthday celebration.

Just as Hugh was backing away from the patio door, he noticed the first car pull into their driveway. The first arrivals were his son Peter and his wife. Within an hour, everyone had arrived and Hugh took his place at the card table. As his grandson shuffled and dealt out the first hand for the evening, Hugh turned to look back at the glass door. The ballerina had finished her dance for one more year in Tyotown Glen.

The new retirement reality

The concept of retirement that we have today is relatively new to mankind. Hugh's grandfather or great-grandfather would not have thought of retirement in the same way as we do today. It would have been a whimsical dream, like flying above the clouds, putting a man on the moon or travelling across the ocean for a week-long vacation in some strange land.

In centuries past, life was very different. Prior to the Industrial Revolution, much of mankind lived in an agrarian society. People worked on the land, not on a production line.

The farm was king, as opposed to cash. Farming, either in the feudal system or on their own land, provided what most families would need to survive. The farm would provide the basis of life.

Money was far less important than owning and working the land. Money could come as an afterthought from selling the surplus of farm production.

The importance of agriculture during this period can be seen clearly in such tragic cases as the potato famines in Ireland and most recently in the Great Dust Bowl Era of the Midwest during the 1930's.

As farms were wiped out, so were families—sometimes with deadly results.

Retirement in past generations was not a concept that could clearly be defined. There was little ability to store up wealth to provide for old age living. Your currency of labour and commodities do not keep over time. People kept working because their lives depended on it, unless they had children who could take over the farming duties.

For many people today, having a garden or an animal is not for the survival of our families but merely as a hobby or to keep in touch with our agricultural past. Today, you will rarely hear stories of self-sustaining family farm activities. These stories are generally of people who we would regard as radicals for living "off the grid". We now require capital before we can attain food. We need cash, not crops, for our city living. Cash is now king.

Retirement in a monetary society provides one distinct advantage, which is the ability to store up wealth. You can develop a clear line between work life and retirement life. The cache of money that can be set aside would not rot or decay as commodities would have in a society of agriculture.

Yesterday's Promise

How many can remember the stories about grandparents who started working at a very early age and had to forego university or college? Their home life required such a sacrifice. There was more of an expectation within society that they should get a job as soon as possible.

Maybe there wasn't enough money to pay for college. Education was no less important to parents and students, but fewer had the luxury of the two most required commodities in order to attend: time and money. For many of Hugh's generation, high school graduation was the successful pinnacle of formal education. Their learning would take place through the classroom of experience and work.

Looking back at the last chapter, we discussed the *personal financial lifecycle*. I was careful not to mention ages or timelines, but I merely stated the different stages. The personal financial lifecycle was applicable in Hugh's life. He learned, earned and yearned. The same phases that Hugh experienced are the same we all face today. What has changed, however, is the duration and timing of each phase, which will continue to ebb and flow over time.

Let us look at what Hugh experienced in timing and phases of the personal financial lifecycle, and we will call this *yesterday's promise*.

For Hugh, yesterday's promise started with a learning phase consisting of about 13 years, give or take a year. He did not go to secondary school, nor did he attend any other formal education after the age of 13. This was not because of a lack of intelligence or laziness that he didn't go to college. Hugh was as bright and intelligent as anyone else, as was proven by his success in business.

Hugh also was far from a lazy individual. Again this was proven in his desire to succeed. The circumstances in Hugh's life, as for many of his age group at the time, just did not allow for this to take place. The boys of his generation were often needed to help the patriarch to support large low-wage families by working the family farm or by working in the city. Time at school was time not earning money.

Of course, the cost to go to school made it more difficult to justify. When some of the more fortunate men his age were able to gain a formal education, Hugh was resolved to get a great education in other ways, even though it would take a little longer.

For Hugh and his generation, the earning phase happened roughly between the ages of 13 and 65. During the early years in this phase, Hugh would slowly build up his annual income and pay down any debts that he might have had. Typical of this part of the personal life cycle, Hugh enjoyed a growing margin in discretionary income and was able to save more for his "golden years", especially after the kids had grown and started their own families. By the time Hugh had reached the age of 50, his income level was at an all-time high and his costs were at an all-time low. He still had more than a decade and a half to accumulate enough assets to provide for the yearning phase.

Finally, Hugh's yearning phase lasted from age 65 until he passed at age 92. This phase was very irregular, as the average man in his generation had a life expectancy of around 75. During that final period of his life, he was able to liquidate assets built up in the earnings phase to provide for his basic needs and lifestyle.

In short, Hugh's personal financial lifecycle consisted of 13 years of learning, 52 years of earning for 27 years of yearning. However, for many of his generation, those periods of time would have been 18, 47 and 10 years respectively.

Think for a moment about how your own family's previous generation has changed. Did your grandparents experience the same societal expectations as Hugh did? Did they also have a life defined by these simple three periods?

This was the timing and duration of the personal financial lifecycle of a not-too-distant generation before us. This was the *promise of yesterday* that was experienced by our fathers, grandfathers and even some of our great-grandfathers.

Today's Reality

There is no question, as Chapter 2 started out, that we are all going to die sometime. Somehow, in some way, on some day, we will go like all great generations before us. In "today's reality", we are just more likely to die at an older age. Today's reality is such that our lives and the expectations for our lives are different than those of "yesterday's promise generation". There has been a paradigm change in the last two generations, built upon how and when our personal financial life cycle phases occur. They still exist, but the phases have become hazy as the duration of each phase has altered.

Over the last two generations, the learning phase has changed. The length of time that individuals are staying in school is longer, as the percentage of high school graduates attending post-secondary institutions have increased. In aggregate, this means that the age at which young people actively enter the labour force occurs later in their lives.

The second thing that has changed is the duration of the earnings phase. At the front end, we have young people entering the labour force at a later age. At the end of the earning phase, we have individuals demanding a retirement much earlier in life. This has caused a *compression* of the number of years that individuals are able to accumulate wealth, as they have to create more wealth in less time.

The average retirement age, although slightly higher in the last few years, is still lower than it was only 25 years ago. This creates a real problem, as the time to accumulate enough retirement assets becomes shorter. Where my grandfather's generation enjoyed 45 or 50 years of working to accumulate savings, many people today demand or expect to have about 30 to 35 years to save for their retirement.

How does this affect retirement planning? Let's look at a basic financial truth in order to understand how significant this change has been.

The accumulation of wealth does not happen overnight. There is no big-bang theory to becoming financially secure—outside of winning the lottery. To accumulate wealth, you need three basic things to exist: money, rate of return and time. In other words, you have to have an amount of money to start with, earn some type of return on it and do it for a period of time. Miss any of these three and you are left with virtually nothing.

Of course, each of these comes with its own set of trade-offs. Invest money now and you give up the immediate gratification of its use. In plain terms, a dollar saved is not a dollar spent. The second variable is rate of return, and this also has a basic historical trade-off. The more return you want, the more risk you will need to assume. The converse is also true: take no risk and you will make no real return.

The last variable, time, is very important, and it is indeed the most important. Time is the greatest ally to investors. The longer the time you have to invest, the less money is needed. The longer the time, the lower the amount of return required (which also means less risk). Time is a diminishing commodity that, once spent, you can never earn back.

The yearning phase has also changed, and it continues to change dramatically. The age that people are passing away is later in life than it has ever been in history. Very simply, people are living longer. In the past, we would die at a much younger age, but now the medical community continues to find ways to allow us to live longer. This means retirement income needs to last for a longer period of time. This factor has exacerbated 'longevity risk' for retirees, which we will talk more about in chapters to come.

When all three changes in the personal life cycle are accounted for, we have a dramatic shift to a shorter period for accumulating wealth and a longer period to provide for in retirement. Hugh's generation had 18 years of learning, while his grandchildren have about 22 years.

Where *yesterday's promise* generation enjoyed around 47 of

accumulation, *today's reality* generation expects to retire as soon as possible after completing only 33 years of work. This means the earnings phase has shortened by 14 years. The yearning years, those years when we must draw on savings to live out the remainder of our lives, has been lengthened by more than 5 years.

To summarize *today's reality*, individuals:

- are going to school longer,
- expect to retire sooner,
- have a compressed period of the time to accumulate sufficient wealth, and
- must build a larger pool of wealth in order to provide for a longer retirement period due to increased longevity.

This is the perfect storm for long-term financial failure, where expectations and dreams are not met with prudent planning.

"People don't plan to fail, they just failed to plan."

CHAPTER 4 ~ FOCUSED FINANCIAL SECURITY

Trinity's story

"What a wonderful Saturday full of promise," Trinity thought to herself as she unlocked the door to open her coffee shop for the day. The cleanliness of the spring morning swept through the entrance of the coffee shop as the borough awoke from its slumber.

The crisp air carried with it the scent of misty dew, freshly lifted by the morning sun from the street and sidewalk. Trinity breathed in deeply, invigorating her senses. She noticed the heavy dew had erased much of the colourful chalk on the sidewalk. Just the day before, the sidewalk in front of her shop had been the battleground for the hopscotch championship of the world, fought by the children living in the apartment above the shop.

Trinity, like she had done for so many Saturday mornings through her childhood, turned the sign around to announce to the world that the *Pantry* was open. The same sign was turned by her great-grandmother when she opened the shop almost 75 years ago. Since then, the shop was passed down to Trinity's mother and, more recently, to Trinity after her mother passed away at the young age of 65.

After pulling up the blinds, Trinity gave a dusting to the sign that hung in the window. She paid special attention to the cranny in the woodwork of the first letter "P". Her great-grandmother, Pearl, opened the shop after emigrating with her husband from Ireland in 1938, looking for a better life and prosperity in North America.

For over 75 years, *Pearl's Pantry* has been a constant fixture for many of the patrons of the borough. Many have known of its existence all of their lives, much like Trinity herself. It became a point of reference for direction-seekers, as well as a place of refuge for countless others.

With the shops sign dusted, it was time for the daily grind.

Trinity's walked behind the service counter, and the coffee grinder began its daily work of turning the roasted Arabica beans into a fine powder. Trinity began to lay out some of the fresh muffins she baked in the wee hours of the morning, just as the first of many customers arrived at the shop.

Mrs. Carpenter had been coming to the *Pantry* for as long as Trinity could remember. At some point early in Trinity's childhood, her grandmother introduced her to the woman for the first time. She was introduced as Mrs. Carpenter, and Trinity as "my little helper". Over time, the formality had dropped, and now they referred to each other as Hope and Trinity.

For Trinity, no matter how young Hope was when she first met, she always seemed to be older. This happens often when we meet older people. They never seem to age at the same rate we ourselves do.

Hope sat in the old dark green leather arm chair that sat opposite an equally-aged red leather loveseat. Between the two pieces sat a lovely coffee table, complete with some light reading, a few trinkets that had lost their space on a shelf and an assortment of cup coasters.

Hope's dark blue spring dress against the backdrop of the red and green furnishings created an artists' palette of primary colours, topped with a frosting of white hair. Hope's age was certainly less than 70, but greater than 65.

Hope did not ask for any coffee at the moment, partly because she knew it was not prepared yet from the sound of the grinder just finishing and partly because her partner for the morning had not arrived.

For the past 27 years, on every Saturday morning that was available, the women would meet for coffee while their husbands went fishing or golfing--or they had some other excuse. They were neighbours for twenty-five years until the Barber family moved a couple of streets away. Now across from Hope and Thomas sat a nice park with a couple of benches and a tall barrier wall, behind which was the widened cross-city road. Prudence Barber and her husband John decided to stay in the neighbourhood, partly because of the close friendship with Hope and Thomas. After all, both Thomas and John were raised there, went to school together and even worked together as carpenters for many years.

Opening time at the *Pantry* was a little after 8am when Prudence arrived. She was always so gracefully gregarious. Hope, who is a self-diagnosed pessimist, liked to call her a 'gregarious' optimist. Prudence was obviously close in age to Hope and carried a positive energy that was contagious. She was never arrogant or conceited, just confident and joyful. If Hope was ever blue, being around Prudence always made the shade of blue a little lighter. The shop was open since 8am, but now it was alive-Prudence was there.

Taking her seat on the red leather love seat that was opposite to Hope, Prudence smiled and waved back at Trinity like a giggly school girl. Trinity, in return, did the same back to Prudence as she watched the first pot of coffee come to completion.

One of the highlights for Trinity over the years was to see these two ladies each week. Their friendship was not bound by economical similarities or any sense of fake friendship. It was a mutual love for each other and devotion to each other's wellbeing. They were the god-parents to each other's first born, and they sat beside each other when parents passed away. Their uncommon relationship was the common ground they both needed.

This day was special. This was the 12th special day between them as a matter of fact. Today, Prudence became a grandmother for the first time, once again. Between Hope and Prudence, they now had 12 grandchildren. Each time a new baby was born, it was a special day for both of them, and with it came the "brag books" which contained all the photos of the grandchildren.

Trinity watched as the two laughed and chuckled over the baby. She brought over to the ladies the usual two black coffees and a plate of assorted fancy sugar cookies. After so many years, there was no order requested or required of the barista.

Prudence was heading to her youngest son's house the next day with John to visit the baby and to spend a few days helping out. It was a 6-hour drive but it was worth it. They would be there to help the new mother, as the father would be returning to work on Monday.

Since John's retirement nearly a decade ago, the Barbers made it a point to do the same for all of their grandchildren. This is something that Hope had always envied, and she secretly wished that her life would have allowed the same freedom. However, Thomas was still working part-time as a carpenter, although his body would probably put an end to that soon.

After the new baby talk had subsided, Hope once again confided to her friend about Thomas' working. It was taking its toll on his health and on his back and knees in particular. They wished to visit their children and grandchildren, but Thomas either had work scheduled or there was not enough money to take time off.

Their financial picture was not as secure as that of Prudence and John. Thomas worked because he had to, not because he wanted to. Hope occasionally would do some work as a seamstress, if it presented itself; however, the beginning stages of arthritis in her hands prevented her from working for any length of time.

Prudence had shared with Hope how their advisor helped them over the years to save a little money each payday and to invest it for the future. Once again, Prudence mentioned to her friend that she should call their advisor. Unfortunately they could never make the call because they both were embarrassed and anxious to discuss their financial situation with anyone.

They never could seem to save any money because there were always things to buy and to do. The house always needed work, the car always needed to be repaired or any number of expenses came up. Thomas and Hope found it hard to understand why they should call someone to help them to invest when there is nothing to invest. So, they never did. They also found it unimaginable that anyone, even Prudence and John, could save money.

The time behind the coffee bar was never slow physically, but there was plenty of time for Trinity to think of the ideas and ponder the discussions that people shared. However, today was a special day. Prudence and Hope unknowingly created a question that, for Trinity, could unlock a secret that would change her life.

Why would two people with such similar upbringings and lifestyles have such dissimilar financial situations? Why would Prudence be able to enjoy freedom and financial security while her friend Hope experienced disappointment and financial stress? How can one family retire while the other must continue to work?

Defining financial freedom

What does it mean to be financially free? It means to have true financial freedom, which includes having abundance as well as peace of mind. In the story at the start of the chapter, why would Prudence and John be more financially secure than Hope and Thomas?

Prudence and John had peace of mind.

Ask yourself this one question: "What do you need to happen in your life in order to be financially secure?"

I have asked this question to many groups and individuals over the past 25 years. Frequently, the answers to this question result in comments such as:

- need lots of cash,
- to have no mortgage,
- to own a house,
- to have a good job,
- to have a high income,
- become older in age,
- get a lucky break or
- win a lottery.

I even once had someone tell me that their financial security is based on how well they marry!

I believe this question crossed both Prudence and Hope's minds on several occasions. On this particular Saturday, it was the first time that Trinity asked herself the same question.

You cannot successfully arrive at a particular destination without first deciding on the destination that you want to arrive at. The same is true with financial security. You cannot arrive at financial security without deciding what that is for you. The first step in achieving financial security is to first acknowledge and define what that actually means.

Man-at-work vs Money-at-work

If you spent any time in front of the television in the early 1980's, you will remember a commercial for a large American donut chain where the opening scene was in a dark bedroom. The bedroom was suddenly brought to groggy life with the alarm clock ringing in the wee hours of the morning.

The character, dressed in armless t-shirt, sat up, turned off the alarm and declared, "Time to make the donuts". Beside him lay his wife, who kept sleeping as the man rose from the bed and stumbled into the bathroom, continuing to say, "Time to make the donuts." This opening scene continued as a loop two or three times. The commercial finally ends with the man, a baker of the donuts, serving customers at the donut shop.

The point of this commercial was to demonstrate the commitment that the baker had so that the donuts were made fresh each morning—well before everyone else had awoken to start their day. As a donut lover myself, I commend him.

The point of this story for our sake is to point out the fact that the man had to go to work. Whether he was committed to his vocation as a baker or he should have been committed as a lunatic, he probably would have preferred to stay home in bed like everyone else.

This, however, was not an option. Every morning, he woke up with a duty in mind. The duty, on the surface, was to make the donuts, but underlying this was the actual material purpose: he needed income. He worked to earn a living to pay for things such as food, clothing, shelter and other personal lifestyle desires of his family.

Of course, this will be a requirement in his life, and in all of our lives, as long as we need income and the only source we have is from our own labours. Therefore, the first source of income to fund our basic necessities and lifestyle is from "man-at-work" activities.

How then can we create a different source of income--a source that does not require us to "make the donuts" each day? How can we stop "man-at-work" activities?

This is simple. We need to create a second source of income to fund our basic necessities and lifestyle by having "money-at-work".

In the same way that we employ our labour to earn money, we can deploy our capital to earn money. Capital which we deploy will earn money, and that money then becomes deployed capital which will also be earning money.

Let's put this in simple terms: Man-at-work earns salary and wages, while Money-at-work earns interest and dividends.

This is the first of the basic truths about financial security. The point at which financial security is achieved is when man-at-work can convert to money-at-work in order to provide for an individual's basic necessities and lifestyle. As long as man-at-work exists because of the lack of money-at-work, an individual does not have financial security.

If you spend a little time thinking about this, you will see that financial security has little to do with any one item on its own. Age is irrelevant on its own, as you can be young or old and still have enough money-at-work to be financially secure (although age has the benefit of time to accumulate).

High income on its own is irrelevant, unless you are able to save a portion of it (although having a higher income will make it somewhat easier to set aside capital for future use).

Having debt or an outstanding mortgage on its own will not remove the chance of financial security (although having less debt means that you have more income to spend from money-at-work).

Even "marrying well" does not guarantee financial security if the spouse does not have money-at-work (although the act of marrying well, I contend, is still a man-at-work activity).

In the story of Hope and Prudence, it is obvious that Prudence was able to build capital through some simple planning so she and her husband could retire. Hope and Thomas, on the other hand, never took the steps to build capital that would allow for them to stop working. He is forced each day to go to work, regardless of the pain he has in his knee and back.

If conversion from man-at-work to money-at-work creates financial security, how can we build a pool of money-at-work when there is little to save? This leads us to the second truth about achieving financial security.

The greatest wealth building strategy EVER is this: PYF! Pay Yourself First!

If I were to ask you to list all of your expenses, could you do it? I am pretty sure you could do it. I am also certain that you could do it with a certain degree of accuracy for most items on your list.

Let's take a moment and try and do this simple exercise. By doing this, it will help you to understand the significance of how we frame and think about our financial lives.

Please list on a piece of paper (and do actually write the list on the paper) all of the items that you spend money on. Give yourself a time limit of 20 seconds. What items or expenses do you have, fun or otherwise, that you spend money on? Where does your money go? As you write them, you will see a list of about 10 or 15 things forming. Once you have completed the list, or once 20 seconds has passed, continue reading.

The list you have built will show things that are very similar to everyone else who has done this exercise. We all need clothing, food and shelter, as much as we need love and acceptance. These are basic needs of the human condition. Further to this, you will have also added lifestyle things, such as bill payments, credit card payments, personal loan payments, transportation items (car payments, gas, insurance), travel, taxes, entertainment, cell phones, hobbies, dining out, charity and a whole host of other items that may be more individual to you.

There is a possibility that you included the monthly savings that you add to your retirement account. Chances are that you did not. There is even a greater likelihood, if you did add it to the list at all, that it did not show up in the first three items.

It is true that I am a wealth advisor for my clients, but not many people know that I also have a special gift of telling the future. This is not for all things, but for one thing in particular, I am going to predict something right here and right now for you personally.

In a few years, maybe in 5 or 10 or 25 years, you will meet someone that you will have a conversation with—a very serious conversation. The individual that you will speak to either will say thank you and shake your hand or will be furious and want to kick you in the seat of your pants.

You might not know it, but you owe them money and they want to collect on the debt. If you have the money, you will be safe and the conversation will be easy. If you can't pay them, they will become angry and you will try to avoid the inevitable conversation.

So, who do you owe this money to? It is you yourself. It is your "future self".

At some point, we all owe our "future self" the future that we both need and arguably deserve. The choice to be happy or angry will depend on your decisions today. What you do today has a dramatic impact on that unavoidable meeting in the future.

You can choose to accept the debt you owe and pay it down now by saving and investing, or you can choose to ignore it and pay the consequences later. No one can choose for you.

Getting back to our list of items that we spend money on, let us consider this debt that we have to our future self. If we choose to ignore it, we will ultimately suffer greatly because of this choice. If we decide to engage this debt, we can learn to pay it off as if it were no different than any other debt.

It should be argued at this point that a debt to our future self and our financial security is more important than many of the other debts or expenses that we carry. We are not talking about owing money to your cell phone company or the subscription to Wood Carvers Monthly. We are talking about YOU!

Not only should we treat it like a debt, we should also put it within the top three items on our list. We need to re-frame how we think about financial security and investing for it. In 5 years, your cell phone will be replaced and it will be worthless. In 10 years, your car will be rusted and completely worthless.

Why do we continue to treat these items, which are items of fancy and not necessity, with such aggressive spending? Sure, we all need transportation and communications in today's society, but we do not need the excess of having the best and newest when we have not paid down the debt to our future self.

In the same way that we owe money on a car loan or a mortgage, we can fix an amount due, the monthly payment and the date when it will finally be paid off. For example, let's say you need to pay off your mortgage of $300,000. The bank sets the monthly payment based on the interest cost and the amount of time to pay it off.

In our example, to pay off a $300,000 mortgage over 25 years at 5% would require a monthly payment of about $1,745. After 25 years, the bank loan is paid off and there is no more debt.

In the same way, we can set the future debt to ourselves of $300,000 to require a certain monthly payment. If we require $300,000 in 25 years with a rate of return of 5%, we would have a certain determinable monthly cost.

This concept is known as Pay Yourself First, or PYF.

In Hope and Thomas's life, they always found it hard to save anything at the end of the month. There was always some expense that came up or something to spend money on that made savings impossible. This is a common problem that many find themselves in.

If we think about it in the context of what we have just read, is this really a "lack of money" problem or a "financial priority" problem? Does the problem exist in their cash flow or does it exist more in the way they have framed the problem to themselves?

If the problem is that there is no money for savings left after paying the bills, maybe the money for savings should be taken off the top first. . . before the other bills are paid. In other words: PYF! Pay yourself first!

In the first few months, it will be difficult to adjust, but something else will have to be sacrificed—probably something far less important to long-term financial health. It might require one less pizza, a slightly lower cell phone plan or one less movie. I don't know what it will be, but something has to be given up so that much more can be gained.

Another way to look at it is from the income side and not just the spending side. If you happen to walk into your work one day and the employer said that the wages were cut by 2% to ensure the longevity of your job, would you die? Would you have to cancel all your subscriptions to Wood Carvers Monthly, cut off your electricity, stop eating, sell the car and sell the cat?

No, probably not. You would adjust to your new reality of an income that is 2% less than before. On a $50,000 year job, this is a difference of approximately $80 per month. Once the new reality is in place, things tend to work out. This is why automatic deductions from employees' wages work so well. It forces employees to adhere to the PYF principle.

This also leads me to mention another, non-tangible benefit of the PYF principle. When we define our financial security, treat it as a debt we will owe to ourselves and then begin to pay down that debt (or build up our pool of money-at-work), we start to become financially self-confident.

Not only does our financial worth become stronger, but our sense of self-worth does also. We confidently move forward without worrying about the future and we become less anxious about spending on certain items.

In the story of Hope, Prudence and Trinity, we find young Trinity questioning the reason for the difference between their financial outcomes--only to discover for herself the truth of financial security. Prudence and John started early to save a portion of their income. Hope and Thomas did not. Prudence and John attained financial security when they were able to convert John's carpentry income into money-at-work income. Hope and Thomas haven't grasped that yet.

"Hope without Prudence is not a strategy."

CHAPTER 5 ~ SAVING, INVESTING AND SPECULATION

Jak's story

The unmistakable sound of the train crossing the back field of the farm could be heard clearly through the windless evening air. It was close enough that every 'clack' sound was distinguishable from every 'clickity'.

"Clickity-clack, clickity-clack", murmured Jak under his voice as he stared at the straw beneath his feet. Jak and his grandfather were taking their evening walk along the lined rows of garlic. The field was as wide as two football fields and long enough that Jak didn't like to walk to the end because he would have to walk all the way back. The sun was about to set and began to wave goodnight to them from the tree tops on the west side of the field.

Jak was all but ten years old. He was an average size for his age with light-brown hair and a few freckles on his nose. Many people said he looked like his grandfather when he was Jak's age.

Like most boys, Jak had as much dirt under his nails and on his face as he had on his jeans and t-shirt. It didn't bother him in the least. His grandmother would see to remedy that before bed. He truly loved coming to the farm each weekend from the city to explore the fields of garlic, play with the barn cats and hide out in the emptiness of the loft.

Jak and his grandfather were walking the fields of garlic that the two of them had planted last October. Jak knew the best time to plant garlic was in the fall just before the ground becomes reacquainted with the winter frost. Having now reached late July, the plants were nearing their maturity, as could be seen by their dark green curling scapes and strong stems.

Jak's grandfather had been growing garlic since he was about ten years old. The farm had been passed down for two generations. Jak was proud of his grandfather who had become known as the Garlic King of Avonmore, the fairly large glen that the farm was in center of. Jak would often peer at his grandfather as he stood tall over the rows of garlic, like a true king overseeing the prosperity of his subjects. They all stood at attention when their king was present. The curly scapes seemed to bow intently before his majesty. Jak wanted to be just like his grandfather when he grew up.

"Grandpa, do you hear the train passing by?"

"Yes, Jak, I hear it. Do you hear the garlic asking for water?" His grandfather replied, looking at the sky and wondering if there might finally be a little rain that evening.

Jak thought that was a ridiculous question, even though he listened to hear if the garlic was truly speaking.

"How many garlic do you think you have?" Jak asked, as he did every weekend that he visited. Jak had been coming to the farm every weekend since the spring thaw. His mother worked on Saturdays in a local shop. Jak had become the careful curator, watching all of the garlics poke through the soil and then start their climb towards the sky.

"Oh Jak, you ask me the same question every week. I have twenty five thousand garlic plants in these three long fields," His grandfather said.

"Did you know that when I was about your age, we only had about a hundred plants and they were along the side of the barn?" Jak's grandfather pointed back towards the big old red barn closer to the house. "These fields were empty and were barely used for anything except for a little hay for the family cow", his grandfather told him.

"Wow," thought Jak. He never knew this before. He always imagined the garlic had always been there since the beginning of time, perfectly rowed by some giant in ancient times.

"How did you get to have twenty-five thousand garlics from only a hundred? Did you have to buy all of them?" Jak inquired, as he wanted to keep talking as they walked. Jak loved to spend time with his grandfather.

"Jak, you know how much you love eating garlic--roasted, pickled or fried. Well, I was just like you. I wanted to eat every garlic bulb that we had. As a matter of fact, I am still like that!"

"I bet you could have eaten all one hundred garlics because I know that I sure could," Jak boasted back to his grandfather.

Jak took a couple of steps and noticed his grandfather had stopped. Jak took two steps back to once again stand beside his grandfather. He noticed that they both wore blue jeans and white t-shirts. He saw that he was wearing the same clothes as his grandfather, except that his smaller set was far dirtier. Jak instantly felt older and more mature.

"Jak, I think you are absolutely correct! Back in the day, I could have eaten every single garlic bulb of the one hundred my father had planted," Jak's grandfather said with certainty, "but what would we have planted that autumn if I had eaten them all?"

Jak thought for a moment. It seemed logical that if you eat every garlic bulb in the summer, there would be nothing to plant in October.

"I don't know Grandpa, maybe you could eat most and save a few for planting", Jak said as he reasoned out loud.

"Jak, that is exactly what we did," his grandfather said as he started to walk a little farther down the row of garlic. "Before any garlic was eaten, my father would select all that he needed to make up next year's planting. These were special bulbs that were not to be eaten, Jak. They were set aside and then carefully planted in October before the first frost."

Jak walked beside him, thinking about this new found logic. Jak remembered his grandmother peeling a garlic bulb in her kitchen that afternoon as she made her famous spaghetti sauce for supper that night. She carefully separated the six individual cloves that made a bulb.

She often would say to Jak that every clove could produce a brand new bulb and each clove could produce six new cloves. At the time, Jak thought that she was talking to herself, but now Jak realized the secret contained in her words. "If this was true," Jak pondered, "then every bulb with six cloves could produce six full garlics, each containing six more cloves. That would be thirty-six cloves!"

"Grandpa, how many garlics did you eat of the one hundred beside the barn each year?"

Smiling as though he was expecting the question from Jak, "Well, let me see," as he put his pointer finger to his temple, "I believe we ate fifty garlics that year".

"Wow Grandpa, that means that you had fifty you did not eat! You must have planted all fifty garlic in the fall," Jak computed proudly.

"Well, I guess you're right Jak, we must've planted fifty," Grandfather replied, knowing his answer was a guess.

Jak quickly corrected his grandfather, "No, Grandpa, I remember Grandma saying that each clove on a bulb produces a new bulb. If there are six cloves to a garlic bulb, you must have had like a million garlic plants!"

"You are quite the mathematician, Jak," replied his grandfather, chuckling lightly. "If we used fifty garlics with six cloves each, we must have had about three hundred plants. Come to think of it, I think that was the year we moved them from the side of the barn to this field, because there were too many plants!"

Jak stopped walking and tried to imagine three hundred garlic plants. "Wow, that was a lot of garlic. It's not twenty five, but it's still lots," he thought.

"Grandpa, how many garlic did you eat that year? Did you eat all three hundred? I don't think I could have eaten that many!" Jak queried as he became noticeably excited at exploring this new found secret.

"I think that year we ate about 75 garlics, Jak. I think that was the year we started selling some of them at the market," his grandfather explained. "If I remember correctly, we selected the first 200 to re-plant, we ate about 75 and we sold the rest at the market.

"So you had 200 to plant!" Jak said with some excitement. "That means that the following spring, you had six times as much! That is like a *gazillion* garlics!"

Jak's grandfather chuckled, "You're almost there, math-genius! I believe we had over 1,200 garlics that year. Again, we kept what we wanted for planting first, we ate what we needed and we sold quite a few that year at the market."

They now had reached the center of the garlic field. The sound of the train was long gone and the sun gave its last goodbye for the day. Jak's grandfather turned and started to walk back towards the house in a parallel row of garlic. Jak came to a stop, staring at the far end of the field. For the first time, he saw the forest more than the trees. Jak finally understood how there were twenty-five thousand garlics in the field and why his grandfather was known as the Garlic King of Avonmore.

Somebody once had to tell you that the air we breathe was all around us. It was all around us from the day we were born, but until someone told you about its existence, you did not know it was there at all. It might have been a parent or a teacher. How many times in your life have you looked so intently trying to see the air?

It is much the same with money and wealth. There are basic truths in life that, once you learn them, it is difficult to ignore their existence. You might not see them, but you know they are true. This book is based on truths—truths that are so absolute and so clear that we frequently miss them entirely, just like the air we breathe.

Let's review the truths discussed so far in this book. The first truth is that we are all going to die someday. The second truth we discussed is that the time we have here on earth is broken into three distinct parts: Learning, Earning, and Yearning phases, each with their own traits.

The third truth lays out the concept that true financial security happens when an individual, or family, is able to convert "Man at Work" income to a level of "Money at Work" income that meets their lifetime needs. The last truth we talked about was that PYF (Pay Yourself First) is one of the simplest and most time-tested wealth building strategies. It is also one of the most important.

These truths are simple. These truths are the foundation to anyone achieving financial happiness. When we understand these basic reasons for planning, it makes the rest of the story much clearer.

In this chapter, I want to expand on some other truisms that seem to be passed over by almost every commentator in the financial media. I believe it is overlooked because it simply isn't sexy enough to sell papers. Let me start by asking the same questions that Jak did.

Can you eat all the garlic you produce? If not, what do you do with the excess garlic?

Sounds kind of funny, but if I exchange the word *money* for the word *garlic*, does it make the question easier to answer?

If we earn $25,000, $50,000 or even $250,000 in a year from work, I will wager that each of us has the natural ability to spend it all. As a matter of fact, this is a talent that many people have fostered and perfected over many years. Let's be more accurate and not call it a talent but a habit. This habit is the most common reason for financial ruin.

In the last chapter we discussed the need to save a portion of what we earn. This was the concept of PYF—Pay Yourself First. The concept basically said this: do not eat all the garlic that you produce, but save some for the future.

Jak learned from his grandfather that he became the Garlic King of Avonmore because he did not eat all that he produced. Jak's grandfather, and his father before him, always kept some for the future right away, and then they ate what they needed and sold the excess. By keeping some of the garlic for the future, Jak's grandfather was using the PYF strategy.

Jak also learned that there is a difference between simply storing the bulbs and breaking them up and re-planting the cloves. If Jak were to simply store the bulbs for future consumption, they would dry out slowly over time and become worthless. If, however, Jak planted the cloves, they would not only live on but they would also grow six-fold. This would not take place over night but over the months to follow.

This is very much the same with our concept of PYF in achieving financial security. If we save a portion of what we make and keep it in cash (as the expression goes, "under our mattress"), it too will slowly dry out and become worthless. How does this happen? It happens because of inflation.

Inflation is an erosion of purchasing power. It is like rust on steel. Slowly, over time, the steel becomes weaker and weaker as the rust slowly gnaws away at its strength until it has no worth at all.

I remember the day that my father came home and declared that he made $30,000 that year. He would go on to explain that his own father probably took 10 years to earn that amount. That was almost thirty years ago when that took place. My father today in the same position would be earning about $60,000 per year. That is double!

This is all fine if the cost of living is the same or is lower than the increase in his wages. Imagine that a common loaf of bread, a simple staple of our diets, had gone up from $1 per loaf to $2.50 per loaf. My father's salary doubled over time but the cost of bread more than doubled. This means that his income does not command the same purchasing power as it did in the past.

This is seen in almost every aspect of life. Bread costs more, cars cost more, houses cost more, and the list continues. It is not uncommon today for a retired senior to say that they paid more for their last car then they did for their first house!

Take this concept into the future. What will be the future cost of things that we need to keep our lifestyle and ensure our long-term financial security? In twenty years, a loaf of bread could easily be $5 per loaf.

If we simply save the money in our mattress, we are allowing our capital to erode like steel. Inflation will chew away at the purchasing power. Ironically, we will go broke by saving! So if saving alone is not the answer, what is?

The act of saving is simply taking a portion of what we earn and setting it aside, using the PYF Strategy. The next logical step is to decide where to set it aside. Now that we have agreed that sticking it under a mattress is not a good idea, we have to choose how to allocate our capital.

When we decide to save, then we ultimately decide to keep money from being spent, and this immediately affects our net worth or Balance Sheet.

A Balance Sheet or Net Worth Statement is a snapshot, like a photo of our family, showing the stuff we own (assets) and the stuff we owe (liabilities) at a particular moment in time. It is called Net Worth because it shows what we would have left over if we sold all of our assets and paid off all of our debts.

When we save money, we should either pay down our debt or increase our assets. Both of these actions increase an individual's net worth.

A good argument against this concept has frequently been, "If I take $30,000 from my income and buy a car with it, will I not have a $30,000 car, which is an asset too?" This is true. If we spend money on any asset, it will show up immediately on our balance sheet.

As a child, the 50cent bag of candy was still worth 50cents, wasn't it? If I take money from my bank account (which is an asset or something I own) and I buy something (another asset or something that I own), do I not have the same wealth? The answer is yes. However, let me explain a major problem with this simple logic and why it has led many down a path of financial despair.

At the point at which I converted 50cents worth of bottles into cash and then I immediately converted it into 50 cents worth of candy, all things are equal. I will say that it probably is, because I never tried to sell candy to anyone once I had it in my hands.

I would argue that once I put my dirty hands in the bag on the store's front step, the whole bag become worth just a little less than the fresh, never-touched items merely 20 feet away in the store. The same can be said about buying a car. When you buy a new car and drive it off the car lot, we all know that it will have lost some of its value immediately. We also know that, over time, the same car will also become worthless. In twenty years, the $30,000 car will become scrap metal.

It is important to understand that there are some assets that will *depreciate* in value over time, and there are other assets that will *appreciate* in value. Two people might have $100,000 in assets. One owns depreciating assets and the other owns appreciating assets. After 20 years, the value of the first will most likely be $0 and the value of the second will most likely be $300,000.

In today's world, the decision to *spend* leads us to accumulate *depreciating* assets and the decision to *save* leads us to accumulate *appreciating* assets.

Financial despair grows over a long period of time when a family tends to focus on accumulating depreciating assets. The family that accumulates depreciating assets feel good about the purchase at the beginning, but they ultimately will have nothing remaining. The other family that concentrates on accumulating appreciating assets will in the short term not feel the same sense of instant gratification, but they will ultimately experience true wealth and prosperity.

Saving vs investing

So, if we spend our time accumulating things that appreciate in value and earn us income, we will grow wealth. This is the basic concept behind "investing".

Saving is simply putting money aside, as in the example of putting garlic bulbs in cold storage. Investing is taking those same bulbs and choosing to plant them in the field, so they will grow and produce more than the original bulb provided.

Of course, the next logical question would be: what types of assets appreciate in value? How can we tell the difference between assets that will grow our wealth versus those that will erode it?

Ask yourself this question: "If I purchase this particular asset, will it be something that I can use and enjoy today or is it something that I must wait and sell later to enjoy?"

If the answer is that by purchasing the asset you get to enjoy the use of it immediately, it will more likely be a depreciating asset. It is an asset that, over time, will erode your wealth and not build it. By using any asset in the present, you slowly erode its value because you are slowly using up its future utility or future usefulness.

For example, if you buy a car, you can drive it right now—and as you use it, its value declines. Even if you buy an antique that is a rare model and worth quite a bit, the only way to ensure the value remains and continues to go up is if you DO NOT use it.

This is what I call the *Rule of Immediate Utility*. It is a rule that determines if an asset will eventually add to personal wealth or take away from it.

The opposite of the Rule of Immediate Utility is what I call the *Rule of Delayed Gratification*. If you do not get some use and enjoyment from the asset immediately, the delaying of this gratification from the asset will often grow its value, so you have an investment. The longer you delay gratification, the longer it will have to appreciate or earn income.

There are some exceptions to the Rule of Immediate Utility and the Rule of Delayed Gratification, but they are very rare. For example, consider a piece of artwork—a particular piece of artwork where its value is solely determined by supply and demand can be an exception to this rule.

If I purchase a rare piece of art, be it a painting or statue, the amount of immediate gratification lies in the eyes or ears of the spectator. Regardless of how much you enjoy it today, it does not decrease in value based on the level of use. You can look at a painting all day and it does not change its value (just don't touch it).

So when we invest, and therefore do not get immediate usefulness, we are creating stores of value. We begin to hold things that will appreciate in worth and even potentially create a cash flow. The more of these items that we accumulate, the more we will advance towards the goal of future financial security.

Eating all of the garlic bulbs results in immediate gratification and immediate utility. Saving it in a cellar would result in a slow decay of the utility of the garlic as it dried and rotted. Re-planting, or investing, a portion of their previous crop back into the ground each Fall would defer the immediate utility of the garlic by creating an accumulating store of value over time.

In the same way, we must use our scarce resource of capital from man-at-work activities.

Investing vs speculation

We have said that the basic concept of investing is to allocate our savings in a way that creates a store of value and initiates money-at-work. This money-at-work provides cash flow. This cash flow is based on the concept of getting monetary consideration by giving up the *Immediate Utility* of our capital. Cash flow that is re-invested back into the investments promotes wealth accumulation.

Investing therefore can be defined as an act whereby the investor attempts to earn a cash flow or income over time as a direct result of purchasing an asset. A secondary result from this activity would be a possible change in value, but is not the primary driver for the activity.

With this concept, we can see that the return on our investment is made up of two parts:

a) The cash flow (interest, dividends or rent) plus
b) Increase (or decrease) in its value.

In other words, the total return on our investment is measured by summing the amount we made in interest, dividends or rent, and adding any increase in its value when it is eventually disposed of. This would be expressed as: Total Return on Investment = Income + Capital Gain.

For example, you invest $100,000 in a rental property that earns $1,000 per month in rent. Assuming that there are no expenses on the property, the total rental income is $12,000 per year. If you sold the property a year later for $105,000, you made $5,000 in capital gain ($105,000 less $100,000). The total return on investment is $12,000 income plus $5,000 gain or $17,000 in total. As a percentage, this would be expressed as 17% ($17,000/$100,000).

The income portion comes from 'money-at-work' in the ownership of the property. It is the benefit you receive since you do not have the immediate utility of or access to your capital. It is important to note as well that cash flow is typically a flow of income from the asset over a period of time. This leads to the conclusion that investing is generally longer term in nature.

The second part of the total return on investment is the *capital gain*. Capital gain is simply how much your capital value went up in value over time. Capital loss is the opposite, describing how much your capital value went down over time. In simple terms for this book, to calculate the capital gain, you subtract your original selling price from your purchase price. The technical jargon used would be: capital gain on a disposition of a capital property equals proceeds of disposition of the capital property, less the adjusted cost base of the property, less any outlays. The meaning of each of these terms can be found outside of this book, because it is the basic concept that I want to discuss.

When we look at a capital gain, it is not an income (such as dividends, interest or rent). It is not a benefit you are earning because you gave up the immediate use of your capital. It is simply a change in the value. A capital gain results when an appreciation in value occurs, and a capital loss occurs when the value depreciates.

What makes a value go up or down? What causes things to be worth more or less? Well, we have to look at a principle of basic economics: supply and demand. The only way something will change in its value in the marketplace is if its demand changes, the supply changes or both. When demand is greater and supply remains the same, the value will be higher. When supply is greater and demand remains the same, the value will be lower.

Shares in companies will increase in value if demand from investors rises. Real estate prices will rise if demand for property ownership rises. The more investors want something, then the more they will pay for it. The opposite will happen if demand falls and creates an excess in supply. The new price will be lower.

Speculation is different than investing by definition. The activity of investing results in cash flow and possible capital gain or loss. Speculation is an activity in which the main purpose is to take advantage of an upcoming change in value.

In other words, Speculation is the attempt to predict the future supply and demand for an asset. You are speculating that the demand will rise, or the supply will shrink, and this will result in a higher market price for a particular asset. There is no expected cash flow outside of this equation. The return will be based solely on the change in value. In other words, total return from speculation will be equal to $0 income plus resulting capital gain.

Many times, people will use the term "investing" to mean both investing and speculating. If someone was to invest in a property that had no building to rent, no crops to harvest or no particular ability to earn income, it would be a venture in speculation. The only profit to be had from owning this vacant piece of land is to sell it at a price higher than the cost to acquire it. Therefore, the only way this can happen is if the demand for the property and the supply around it changed.

Other examples of speculative assets are gold, precious metals, commodities, art and collectibles. All of these things provide no offspring in the form of income. They simply sit, and the value changes with the markets supply and demand. Changes are either up or down.

To invest means taking our capital and allocating it to earn income by 'money-at-work'. We plant garlic as Jak's grandfather did to reap a harvest of more garlic. If he simply stored the garlic and hoped the supply and demand for garlic changed, then we are speculating.

Investing is generally a far less risky venture than pure speculation, simply because we are paid an income and we recapture our cost over time. Speculating means that if the supply and demand remain the same, then the value of the garlic would fall as it decayed. All things being equal, when we consider assets such as gold, precious metals, commodities, art and collectibles, the only increase we can count upon results from price inflation.

Jak's grandfather increased his yield by always saving and investing a portion of his harvest back into the ground. He knew slowly and surely that this would increase his wealth. He did not speculate in owning the land but instead he cared about the crop that he nurtured. Over time, the value of his land kept up with inflation, but it was his investment in garlic crops that made him the Garlic King of the Avonmore Glen.

What are you doing to increase your financial harvest?

CHAPTER 6 ~ CAPITAL MARKET HISTORY: OWNERS VS LOANERS

Sarah's story

Sarah, now 39 years old, had decided a few years back to take over a business where she had worked faithfully for 15 years. The previous owner and mentor, who had become a close personal friend, had retired after founding the store some 30 years before. Sarah always joked that she traded in 8 hours a day of work as an employee for 15 hours a day as a business owner. She liked dealing with customers at the store but today was not one of those days.

The store was located on the main street of her small vibrant town. The store sat comfortably between a small cafe and a flower shop boutique. Over the past 25 years the store became a fixture in the community. It was known for its excellent customer experience. Sarah was proud of this as she was instrumental in some changes over the past fifteen years that turned the store into such a success.

As Sarah crossed the street she noticed her former mentor and friend, sitting in the window of the little restaurant. The restaurant was more of a greasy spoon. It was a simple place that offered a good breakfast and hot coffee at a fair price. Nothing fancy with the lone exception of its great servers. Sarah liked it there and decided she would pop in for a coffee with her former employer and friend.

Ike Thompson had chosen his usual seat against the window where he would often sneak away to have more private conversations with customers or friends—which often were not mutually exclusive. This was the same table they sat at when Ike first hired Sarah and the same table that saw the ownership of the shop change to her over a handshake. Ike was now well over 70 years old with silver streaked hair and recently started to walk with a cane.

He was very much liked in the community both as a businessman but also for his involvement in local charities. It was not uncommon for Sarah to come in to the shop each morning and see her friend still adhering to his long habit of the morning visit to the café.

Ike waived Sarah over to join them. Ike was not alone. The owner of the flower shop, Erica, was also sitting there having a coffee before she would open her shop for the day. Ike and Erica's conversation halted as Sarah approached to take a chair at the table. The four sides now were occupied by Ike, Erica, Sarah, and the window looking out onto the main street.

"Good morning Sarah", Ike and Erica said at the same time as Sarah removed her coat.

"Good morning folks. I can see the world's problems are being handled quite well this morning with you two", Sarah replied jokingly.

A waitress quickly came over and joined in with a smiling morning greeting. "Did you want a coffee this morning Sarah? We also have a wonderful fruit salad if you are hungry."

"Yes please; but just the coffee. I think I will need it this morning", Sarah replied.

Ike and Erica looked at each other and quickly changed the topic from their previous conversation.

"What seems to be the problem this morning", Erica asked.

"Let me guess," Ike jumped in, "you have problems with that front door lock or is it Mrs. Braniggan's cat digging in your garden again?"

"No, I need to meet with the bank this morning to change the business loan", Sarah said "and you know how much I dislike this". Sarah wanted to increase her loan as a business opportunity had come up for the store and would need some extra capital to purchase equipment and supplies.

"Ah," Ike could only reply. He remembered those days not too long ago. "I am glad it is you and not me! I am retired!"

"Well, one of my employees would like to talk today about a possible raise in her wages, and you know how much I find these conversations uncomfortable", Erica shared.

The waitress placed a white porcelain cup and saucer in front of Sarah and confidently poured the coffee. After filling Sarah's cup, the waitress topped-up Ike's and Erica's coffees before heading to the next table.

"I am sure the bank will lend me the money, but I feel like a needy child when I ask them for a loan. I am the one taking the business risk, and all they care about is protecting their loan," Sarah said sheepishly.

"The bank is a fair weather friend at best, Sarah. They only want to lend money to those who really shouldn't need it! It is a strange thing, it is. The safest loans they can make are to those that on paper shouldn't be asking in the first place." Ike said as he wiggled his fat finger in the air.

"Yeah, but what options do I have?" Sarah asked.

"Well, you could always ask someone else to become an owner and invest in the business with you", Erica answered. "I looked at doing this but decided against it last year. I would have had to share my profits with them and they would get some say in how I run my business. Imagine that! I don't mind sharing a coffee, but not my profits!"

Erica continued, "The one good thing was there was no need to repay them as it is not a loan."

"This is true Sarah" Ike agreed with Erica. "Having other owners would be one way to help finance the business but you would have to share ownership decisions and profits".

"I had thought about that but think a loan is the best option. Especially if I can borrow money at 4% and make 20% on the investment in the business". Sarah smiled pretending to rub her hands like a greedy old miser.

"Gee, Ike I think Sarah is imitating you!" Eric jumped in. "Sarah, the business that Ike started and you took over already is making a tonne of money. You have a monopoly in our market, you greedy blonde beauty!" Erica joked.

"Monopolies come and go and a business needs to forever change and adapt", Ike reminded the women. "Sometimes this requires change and change at times needs to be financed".

Ike Thompson once again raised his chubby pointer finger. "Over the long term, monopoly or not, a successful business owner will always do better than the lender that lends to them. It is inevitable. The costs of business must be lower than the revenue—maybe not every year, but surely over time."

There were a few seconds of silence as both Erica and Sarah knew Ike was not done with his finger wag.

"Did you ever notice that the game of Monopoly is only made by one company, strange thing that is." Ike finally said to break the silence.

"Do you look in the mirror in the morning and practice this verbal garbage Ike?" Erica laughed.

"Erica, your situation is no different. You have an employee that wants a wage increase and you are concerned for the same reason as Sarah". Ike turned to face Erica.

Ike's chubby finger was now like a puppet and Ike was the ventriloquist. Maybe it was the other way around. Sarah and Erica watched the talking finger as much as they looked at Ike Thompson.

"A successful business owner can NEVER pay an employee what they generate for a business regardless how great they are—never. A strange thing, that is." Ike and his finger declared. "Imagine if you paid them what they generated? Where is the profit in that? In the same way, if you paid the bank the same amount as the revenue you earned, you would not have a business profit. An employee is a leverage tool to greater profit."

"Well that is callous, Ike" Erica said.

"Don't confuse pay, worth, and profit", Ike clarified. "There must be a profit in the venture of hiring someone or it becomes a worthless venture and the business will ultimately fail. That does not mean that you are not paying and rewarding them for what they are worth. They simply must be paid their worth. There is nothing more important to a business than its stakeholders. If you pay someone per hour, the profit from their labour must be at least some number greater than that amount per hour.

"This is no different than Sarah wanting to embark on a business project and wanting to borrow money at a lower rate than the expected revenue. Over the long run, the return to lenders of money or labour will be lower than the return to owners who engage them."

"Wait a minute," Sarah interrupted, "you mean to tell me that you profited off my labours for the past 15 years?"

"It is a strange thing, that is!" Ike replied as he lowered his puppet finger and quickly took a sip of his coffee.

There is no arena like the capital markets where history repeats itself with such accuracy, ferocity and frequency. So often, it is the same circus coming to town but just with different clowns. What has happened in the past will continue to happen again in the future. True short-term risks are offset by long-term benefits for those who understand history. Great businesses thrive. This is one of few certainties that the capital markets can offer.

If capital market history repeats itself, is there something that we can learn to help us succeed? The answer is absolutely, and without fail, YES! This chapter is all about what capital markets are and what history has shown us about them.

What is a capital market?

This chapter is not meant to resemble your college financial textbook filled with definitions to memorize. I would not subject anyone to that torment unless they were in one of the classes that I teach.

Understanding various terms within the financial industry can be paramount to success in your own personal finances, regardless of how nauseating it can be. How can you possibly make wise choices without first understanding the opportunity or risk which is placed before you? Luckily, many of the terms and acronyms can be learned quite quickly if we keep things simple.

In my daughter's elementary dictionary, the term "market" is defined as a place where people meet to buy and sell goods. The term "capital" simply means money. From this, we can simply say that a capital market is a place where people meet to exchange money for some other form of financial asset. It is no different than saying that the vegetable market is where vegetable sellers meet with people who want to buy their vegetables. The capital markets are places where people who have money to invest or lend go to meet people who require investment capital. The term "capital market" is an umbrella term that describes all markets where money is exchanged for some type of investment.

Under the capital market umbrella, you will find these three basic markets: the money market, the bond market, and the stock market. The first two markets are where people go to borrow and lend money. The stock market, on the other hand, is where people go to exchange capital for ownership in businesses.

Trading on the money market, you will find things like treasury bills, banker's acceptance, finance and commercial paper. These items all have one thing in common and why they are considered to be money market items. They all have a maturity period that is less than one year. In other words, if you lend money to the government in exchange for a treasury bill (also known as a T-bill) you will be repaid in either 90, 180 or at the most 360 days, depending on the maturity you choose. It is really like a short-term loan or a formalized "IOU".

Items trading on the bond market are loans where a business or government borrows money in exchange for a bond (i.e. a written promise to repay). These bonds are loans that have a maturity period of more than one year. It may be 5 years, 10 years or even 30 years. As a bond is a contract between the lender and the borrower, there can be any number of funky variables or features that would either entice a lender or benefit the borrower. Until maturity, when the bond must be repaid, the borrower will pay an amount of interest for the debt.

The last market under the capital markets umbrella is the stock market. This is simply a market where people who want to invest in businesses exchange with people who want to sell shares in a business. It is nothing more than that, no matter how sexy and complex the media and Hollywood want to make it seem.

These three submarkets make up the larger capital markets, and they have been in existence for many years in ever-evolving forms. We can trace capital markets back centuries in history. From this empirical evidence over hundreds of years, through countless business cycles, wars, famines, global economic powerhouse shifts and economic bubbles, there are some very interesting and solid theories that can be learned from this study.

Ownership vs loanership

When we look over longer periods of time, the various components of capital markets offer some clear evidence of three basic lessons:

a) Owners outperform loaners
b) Investors are rewarded for assuming a specific diminishing risk
c) The greater the risk you accept, the greater the potential return

In a previous chapter, we talked about there being only two ways to earn an income (man-at-work and money-at-work). We also discussed that there are only two things you can do with income (spend or save).

Now, we come to yet another two-some rule; there are only two ways to invest: ownership or loanership. In other words, you can either take ownership in something or you lend money to someone who will themselves take ownership.

We will call this latter way to invest "loanership".

When you lend money, you are still considered an investor, as you have given up your immediate utility to money for some future benefit that is greater. Lending money can be as simple as when we deposit money in the savings account at the bank, because it is a loan to the bank who will in turn re-lend it at a higher rate of interest.

Lending can also be done when we invest in bonds that are issued by various businesses or governments. Again, we give up the immediate utility of the capital in hopes of earning interest income. Further to this, we can also lend money in the form of a mortgage to someone who would like to buy a house or building. As the mortgage lender, we again will earn interest. In all of these cases, the loan will need to be repaid and we would get our original capital back. These are all loanership investments.

Ownership investments are those allowing you to have full rights to the unlimited earning potential of the investment as a trade-off for your absolute risk of capital loss. If the investment does well, then you do well. If the investment does excellent, then you do excellent. If the investment suffers losses, you suffer losses. This does not occur to the same extent as with loanership investments. Typical examples of ownership investments are real estate and shares in companies.

Capital Market history

Over longer periods of time, *ownership* outperforms *loanership*. Ownership investments have a higher average annual return on investment than all loanership investments. In other words, if you invest in an ownership-type asset, you should do better financially than the person who lent you the money for the purchase.

Let me give you an example. A person who lends money to a business should, over the long term, have a lower return than the amount of the business' revenues and should therefore earn less than the business owner. It would not make sense that the business over a long period of time would generate revenue lower than the rate of cost on the debt. The business would ultimately become bankrupt.

The mortgage lender of a piece of real estate should have a lower return on investment than the real estate owner for the same reason. The real estate investor would never have taken on the investment in order to lose money.

Another truth about capital market history is that the short risk associated with ownership investments is greater than loanership investments. For those who have done any athletic training, you will know this expression: *No Pain, No Gain.* With investments, the expression is this: *No Risk, No Reward.*

We have talked about the capital markets consisting of three particular parts: money market, bond market, and the stock market. I described the first two as markets between lenders and borrowers. The latter is a market consisting of business ownership. To simplify this discussion, we can refer to these three capital market parts: cash, bonds and stocks.

The historical characteristics of these three capital market parts are pretty clear, and this will help investors to make wise choices about their investments.

I could easily demonstrate the historical returns and risk between each of these areas, but I choose not to do that right now for a few basic reasons. First, the mission of this book is to offer easy-to-understand concepts that are practical in their application and founded on common sense.

Other than a few anecdotes, a bunch of statistical data would only take away from the simplicity of the writing, adding no lasting benefit to the reader.

Second, the explanation of the data would become confusing and overwhelming, and it would put most sane people to sleep. I prefer that you read the whole book and not have a brain injury halfway through the contents.

Lastly, anyone can find or manipulate statistics in order to achieve their intended goal. I am sure that there is a statistic that proves this, too. The truisms about capital market history are apparent and can be found without looking too deeply for evidence.

Over the past 200 or so years, we can examine the risk and return of the three capital market parts. We can break them down into periods of time, such as any period of 1, 5, 10, 20 or 30 years. These are important breakdown periods simply because they reflect what most people experience and think of in terms of short-term, medium-term and long-term financial time horizons.

When we break the three capital market parts (stocks, bonds, and cash) down into these time frames, there are some clear historical correlations between risk and return. In other words, over different periods of time, investors would have experienced recognizable results.

Before we go any further, let us quickly discuss the two basic variables: risk and return.

What is risk?

Risk means different things to different folks. If I were to ask you what risk means to you, you will probably have the following answer: "Risk, to me, is when I can lose my money."

This is really an answer without definition, even though it seems like a pretty straight forward answer.

I have yet to meet anyone who would like to lose any of their money; however, loss comes in very different forms. There is short-term loss and long-term loss. There is absolute loss without recovery and temporal loss with potential for recovery. There is opportunity loss and also purchasing power loss. Risk is a loaded word and it can be used in many different ways.

For the most part, risk is scary. Here is an example of that. One day, when my daughter was about 4 years old, I found myself (as usual) parked on the sofa and watching a baseball game on television. My wife was out, and I stayed back home with my daughter. Later in the evening, it was time for my daughter to get to bed. Her bedroom was down a long hallway that I could clearly see from the sofa I was sitting on. I told my daughter to head down the hall and get into bed and that I would be there to tuck her in after the next inning had finished.

At first, my daughter started down the hallway with a certain skip in her step, which slowly became a tip-toed creep. The living room had lights on, but the hallway and her bedroom did not. As she went down towards the room, the light slowly became darkness. By the time she reached her doorway, she stopped, turned and ran back to me. "Daddy, it is dark and I am afraid of the dark."

The ballgame was at a climactic part, but my daughter obviously did not want to head down that hallway without me to protect her. We sat and watched the last minute of the inning and then I carried her down to her bedroom. I explained that there were no boogie-men under her bed that were hoping to drag her into some unknown abyss.

As I entered her room with her in my arms, I turned on the light and explained that it was the same room, but it was only void of any light. Nothing was different. To her, I looked like a hero. To me, I quickly understood how clients thought about risk.

I could enter the room with confidence because I had done so for many years. When I was her age, I too was afraid of a dark room. For me, it was where Big Foot lounged around, waiting to chew on my skinny bones. Over time and with experience, I drifted from the fear of the dark because I came to realize the truth (but in truth, I was always thinking about Big Foot).

One of the greatest deterrents to investment decisions is the fear of losing money because of a poor decision. At worst, it is the fear of complete loss of our money. A second deterrent is the fear of a short term set back without the confidence to know that we will earn it back.

Our past experiences, or lack of experiences, help to dictate our comfort level and our tolerance of risk. The more we learn and understand the truth about risk, then the less that certain types of risk will affect us. This occurs in many areas where we may never have had experience before: flying, travel, marriage, children and even death. Today, my daughter is a healthy and happy lover of all rooms, regardless of the light, but I am hopeful that she still thinks of the odd boogie-man and needs her dad to protect her.

For the purpose of this chapter, I will speak of only two types of financial risk: short-term risk and long-term risk.

Short-term risk is a concept that everyone, without exception, has to deal with. It is the potential that in any given period, be it 1 day, 1 week or even 1 year, that the value of our money will become less or even disappear completely. This short term risk is debilitating. It creates, more often than people want to admit, an inaction. It is the short-term potential dissatisfaction of making a bad decision, not matter how logical it seems to be to meet a goal. For many who might lack investment experience, there is a sense of "cross my fingers and jump".

There is an adage, "Going broke safely", that has been bounced around the financial industry for decades. This is long-term risk. It became very popular during the 1970's and 1980's when inflation started to really encroach on people's purchasing power. The long-term risk is that the same dollar will not keep pace with inflation, resulting in an absolute loss of purchasing power.

This is a concept that can be hard to imagine for some people. To help to explain this, let's say that you have two $100 bills in your hand, and it is the only $200 you own. You deposit one $100 bill into your sock drawer, and with the remaining $100 bill you decide to take your spouse out for supper and a movie, and then you stop at your favourite café afterwards. The total cost for the night out was $100 exactly. An enjoyable night with your spouse is well worth the $100.

Ten years later, you happen to be cleaning out your sock drawer and you come across the long-forgotten $100 bill. You remember the great time that you both shared last time, and you decide to repeat the evening out. You go to the same dinner, the same theatre and the same café.

The problem becomes apparent when you find out that your $100 bill is completely spent on the dinner and movie only. There is nothing left for your favourite café. In other words, the cost of everything has gone up, but your $100 bill remained a nominal value of $100.

This is the long-term risk associated with investing. The risk involves the possibility that the value of the investment will not keep up with the increase in prices.

Short-term risk is quantified by a term called *standard deviation*. Long-term risk of capital is measured by what is known as the *real rate of return*.

If there was ever a term that made non-financial people become sick to their stomachs it is standard deviation. The term is not something that we would use in everyday talks without us looking like a weirdo.

The term however is not restricted only to finance. It is used in many statistical calculations and metrics. It also is not hard to understand if academia stopped trying to make it so technical.

To deviate is simply how much something is different from the normal or average. If we think of deviant behaviour in people, we see people who are different than an average person. The greater the difference from the average, then the weirder or more deviant they are. It is the same with statistics.

If the normal is the average, we can see how much something else deviates from it. We can then come up with some basic standardization that allows a comparison between two or more things.

When we look at risk from an investment point of view, we can determine what an average return is for an investment over a period of time, such as stocks, bonds or cash. We can then see how much a given year deviates from the average. The greater the deviation, then the greater is the short-term risk.

What is the rate of return?

When we look at rate of return on an investment, we are looking at how much we are making in total over a certain time period by holding the asset. This is a combination of two distinct parts: the amount of cash flow we earn and the change in value (positive or negative).

For example, the total return on a real estate rental property is the net rent received plus the change in the value of the property itself. If we invest in shares of a business, it is the combination in the dividends from the business and the change in the value of the shares. All investment returns are made from these two important parts.

The real rate of return is simply what is left after you take the rate of inflation off the total return of the investment. For example, if an investment made 8% total return (including both the cash flow and the appreciation of value) and inflation was 3%, this would yield a real rate of return of approximately 5%.

Over time, the total rate of return might be positive, but after inflation is figured into the equation, the result could easily be a negative return.

If the result is a negative of 3%, an individual's capital will be worth one half of its current value in 24 years. This is called "going broke slowly". You would be better off spending it.

Is there relationship between risk and return?

An investor is rewarded for taking on risk, and so the greater the risk, the greater the reward or return over time. Owners outperform lenders, but not without the short term risk of loss.

If we are to agree that you must be rewarded as an investor for taking on risk, there must be some baseline that defines the reward and risk level. There must be some fundamental starting point.

The fundamental starting point would be any investment that had "no risk", and the return on this would be the basic starting point from which all investments add the return in order to justify the risk. In other words, what investment has virtually no risk?

Many times, I have put this question to groups or classes that I have instructed, and the typical answer to this question is: money in the bank. Is this true, though?

It is true to say that the money on deposit in a Canadian Chartered Bank is guaranteed by a federally-incorporated Crown corporation. This means, indirectly at least, that the government will guarantee the deposit of the account holder in the institution. For this to occur, the institution itself must pay premiums to a fund and maintain certain cash levels. The deposit level of the guarantee is also limited to a certain dollar amount.

On the surface this would seem like a safe investment; however it is not an investment that is truly without risk for the investor.

There is another investment called a Treasury Bill, or more commonly referred to as a T-Bill. It is a short-term obligation or loan that the government must repay to the lenders (who are usually citizens and residents of the country). This investment is part of the money market within the capital markets. In short, the government borrows money to meet its short-term needs and it promises to repay the debt in either 90, 180 or 360 days.

Let us think about which of the two has the greater level of guarantee? If the bank was to experience a possible default in Canada, there is a great chance that many of the banks would experience the same level of distress. The government would need to sure up the banks and the banking system, but only after making sure that it is able to meet its own obligations.

If there is a shortfall in the funds required to meet its obligations and to pay off its lenders (the citizens), it can raise taxes (on its citizens) to pay them off. In other words, if they need to pay us back a dollar, they could simply raise our taxes and collect the dollar to give back to us. It is a tremendous purchasing power that the banks do not have.

When we consider the basis for the extra reward that we must receive as an investor, we need to look at the basic investment that carries (in theory anyway) virtually no risk or is considered risk-free. From this risk-free investment, we can determine how much more return must be expected in order to accept a certain amount of added risk. How much reward will we get for the added risk? This is called the *risk premium*.

If the risk-free rate of return on T-Bills is 3%, then any investment with any risk must offer a potential of more than 3%. The greater the risk, the greater the return over the risk-free investment return.

This makes sense when we use another example to push the concept a little further. Let us say, for example, that Investment A and Investment B have the same amount of risk. In other words, they have the same amount of potential loss. The return on investment A is 10%, whereas the return on Investment B is only 5%. Based on this information alone, which would you choose? Unless you are a crack-addict, you would pick the one with the greater return if the risk is the same.

As an investor, we want guarantees. We all want the greatest return for the least amount of risk. History, as shown by the capital markets, does not allow for this. In order to generate high returns over the long run, more short-term risk must be accepted. The amount of risk we accept must produce an adequate risk premium reward in order to justify the risk.

What capital markets have shown allow us to tailor our investment portfolio to meet our individual needs and financial goals. The next chapter will look at how to take advantage of capital market history while building your investment portfolio.

CHAPTER 7 ~ THE INTELLECTUAL FRAMEWORK

Alexander's story

Alexander made his way up the walk to the merchants building where he worked as a clerk, being careful not to slip on the wetness of the cobblestone. The grey stone building was the only two-story building that sat along the quay.

As Alexander approached the building, he noticed the cornerstone was a different shade of grey than the rest of the building. Behind the mason's mark and date of 1518, he could see that the stone had four distinct hues. He never noticed this before. Each corner of the stone had a distinct shade of grey but melted perfectly into each other as they all met at the centre. What a fitting stone for the job, he thought, as he opened the great wooden door and went inside.

Alexander was only 20-years-old and came into the position of clerk with a German merchant known as *Fuggar the Rich*, because of his father being a ship's officer upon one of the company's carracks. Alexander's sister Elizabeth also worked as a keeper of accounts. Their father made learning to read, write and maintain a sufficient study in mathematics a priority. It paid off when Herr Fuggar was in need of personnel for his company's new dockside office in Limerick.

The brother and sister worked on different floors within the building and would see each other at lunch. They frequently took lunch together just outside King John's castle or along the bustling docks, watching company ships being unloaded with trade from the continent. The ships would sail to and from the great ports in England, Spain and France.

THE INTELLECTUAL FRAMEWORK

Today they planned on enjoying their oatcakes and cheese along the docks as three Fuggar ships were expected to arrive. The ships were carrying wine from Bordeaux, wool from Wales and fine linen from Italy. It had created a stir in the small city upon the Shannon estuary, as these luxury items only arrived once or twice in a year.

Irishtown, the small poor village containing Irish and Danes just outside of Limerick, is where Alexander and his younger sister called home for the past ten years. The thatched roof hobbles were little more than garden sheds compared to the grand stone buildings within the limits of Limerick.

This was not what their father had intended for his family. A long-time seaman, he once owned his own merchant carrack and had a thriving business, transporting goods from Scotland. It was thriving until, on one fateful night, a fire in the harbour resulted in his ship being lost. All the family's wealth went up in the smoke within a few hours. All they could do was watch from the same quay that Alexander and Elizabeth now worked at. It was after this tragedy that Jakob Fuggar, the wealthy German, employed their father in the Fuggar fleet.

Alexander removed his cap and sat at his desk. There was much to do as a clerk with the arrival of these three ships. Before arrival, he would make sure that all of the accounts of the arriving goods were in order, so that easy inventory could be made as the cargo was unloaded. If things were not prepared in advance, there would surely be many items that might find their stolen way through back alleys and onto other smaller boats, bound for resale somewhere else.

Alexander was meticulous, as his father taught him to be about keeping accounts. Herr Fuggar was seldom in the Limerick office, as he had offices all across the continent where he would visit and spend time at. His favourite time in Limerick was the Fall, and with this being early October, Alexander found Herr Fuggar at his desk each morning just before sunrise.

His father might have taught him a thing or two about keeping accurate accounts, but Herr Fuggar was teaching Alexander other important things about being a merchant. Herr Fuggar took an interest in Alexander, with his knack for keeping clean accounts and his common sense approach to business. Jakob Fuggar could foresee a time in the near future when Alexander could possibly oversee all of the Limerick activities.

On this particular day, as they were working towards the midday hour, Alexander came across an unusual record of each ship's cargo. It seemed that each ship contained in its hull one third of the total amount of the wine, one third of the total amount of wool and one third of the total of fine linens. Why would this be? Why not put each of the three items upon one ship? Could this be a mistake?

Alex grabbed ledgers and journals from previous arrivals for the Fuggar ships. To his amazement, each of the arrivals in years past had the same allocation to the various ships. Alexander scratched his head in wonder, but he realized that he better get back to the task at hand and not dilly around with unnecessary issues.

The air outside was salty and fresh. The smell of the ocean was combined with smells of fish and produce as Alexander and Elizabeth walked along the quay past the mongers and panhandlers. As they walked, they heard the stories from the seas. Glory and treachery were in every tale.

One fish monger was certain a giant sea monster had swallowed a merchant ship that was past due to arrive. Another dock runner was talking excitingly about a score of four ships: two were lost to the terrible storms in the Irish Sea, and two made a triumphant and profitable arrival in Dublin. Alexander and Elizabeth could not tell if the stories were sailors' tall tales or if they had any truth at all.

The Fuggar Company carracks were now safely at dock. Alexander and Elizabeth were certain of this, regardless of the tales. The unloading would begin in the next few hours after Mr. Rielly, the customs master, reviewed each ship and their holds. He was a small man, but not many a man gave him much sass for fear that they would find themselves picking up their front teeth from the wooden planks. Mr. Rielly was about collecting customs taxes and not about making friends. He also was not interested in listening to your story. It was probably the reason why he never married.

As Alexander and Elizabeth sat with their legs dangling off the quay wall and ate their oatcakes, Mr. Rielly walked by behind them along the dock to Fuggar's boats.

"Good day to you, Mr. Rielly," Alexander said.

"Grrr, what is so good about this day?" he grumbled as he walked past. "Same as every other day."

After Mr. Rielly passed by, Alexander shared with Elizabeth what he had discovered that morning. Elizabeth could not answer her brother's question nor quell the need for him to get the answer. They both agreed to ask Herr Fuggar after lunch. There has to be a reasonable explanation why he divides his goods between the ships.

Returning to the office earlier than expected, they found Jakob Fuggar still at his desk. He had not moved since his arrival that morning.

"Herr Fuggar, sir, may I bother you for a moment?" asked Alexander as he came through the front door. Elizabeth had already put her jacket on the hook and was walking towards her desk at the back left corner of the building.

"What is it, boy? You can see I am working, can you not?" he snorted back.

Before Alexander could ask his question, Herr Fuggar jumped in. "Very well then, I lost my train of thought. Have at it, then."

"Well, sir, I was accounting for the cargo that we are expecting in the carrack's holds and I found something odd," said Alexander in a low voice.

"Well, what did you find? Do we have a couple of unwanted castaway rats from England aboard?" Herr Fuggar laughed, amused by his joke.

"No, sir. I am sure that it is not a mistake but merely an oddity that I would like to understand," the young man said, now with a little more confidence.

Herr Fuggar's voice became serious again.

"Let me solve this for you straight away. The assortment of arms and blades are not part of the cargo that needs to be reported. They are for our friend, the Earl of Kildare. No one needs to know about this small private collection, understand?"

"Herr Fuggar, I assure you, I know nothing of any gift for the Earl Fitzgerald," Alexander said with his hands up in a stopping motion. "I merely ask why each ship would contain one third of each item being brought to Limerick, sir."

Jakob Fuggar's face returned to its normal serious self as he walked to the window, looking out at the quay. "Come here, boy," he said. "Do you see the three ships bearing both our flag and that of Limerick?"

Alexander walked across the planked floor and stood at the window with Herr Fuggar. "Yes, all three of the ships are lined up and ready to unload the cargo in their holds."

"I see wealth and profit," Jakob Fuggar said. "I see wealth and profit, but I also see loss."

Alexander did not understand, and the bend in his eyebrow gave his confusion away.

"You see, boy, these three ships all contain my wealth. When they are at port, there is little that can happen. When they are at sea, well, we can ask your father, if you prefer."

Alexander knew that this is one of the moments when he just needed to keep quiet and listen.

"If we put all of my wealth into one ship, and that ship is lost, so is my wealth. One storm, one fire, one pirate or one of a multitude of possibilities, and my wealth is gone. If I cast my wealth amongst many ships, then losing one ship, although unfortunate, would not lead to financial ruin." Herr Fuggar explained it as if he had done it many times before with other clerks.

"I do not know with certainty what storms are brewing, and neither does anyone else. Some people claim to know the weather by some proprietary science, but they have been wrong so often. I have a logical plan that I implement, regardless of the weather forecast, stories of piracies or potential for fire. I divide my cargo amongst my ships. In the same way, I divide my other wealth. This is by design, and it safeguards against happen chance.

"When you sit along the quay wall with your sister, did you ever notice that the ships in the harbour tend to rise and fall with the tide?" he continued his explanation.

"Of course, it is a slow rise with the riptide, and a slow decline with the ebbtide," Alexander stoically replied as Elizabeth nodded her head in agreement.

"Very good, boy," Herr Fuggar said, celebrating with the boy. "So, as only God can command the moon, we must accept the tides."

Jakob waited a moment to let the comment sink in with Alexander, and then he continued. "We might have to accept the fluctuations of our ships because the tide will do what it wants. I say to you, only a fool would risk having all his wealth in one boat, whether sitting in the harbour or upon the sea.

"By logical design, we will succeed Alexander. You will succeed. It will not be by making short-term guesses based on opinions, forecasts or your own emotions. Truly, I tell you to let logic triumph over emotions."

Alexander finally understood why all of Herr Fuggar's wealth was not contained in only one ship. "It makes me happy that you asked such a question, Alexander. I think you are starting to learn a few things from this Ole Merchant after all!" he said laughingly. "You better get back to work, boy."

"Thank you, sir!" Alexander responded.

Alexander was just about to return to his desk when he laughed and said to Herr Fuggar, "Maybe, sir, someone will write a play one day about your merchant stories and your naval theories!"

Jakob looked up from his ledger, "Aye, maybe, just maybe. Alas, I fear it will not be the wealthy German Merchant of Limerick. As all things seem to go, it will most likely be some English bard penning a romantic play concerning a merchant in a romantic Italian city! It is doomed to failure, surely!"

The noise

Every day, new reports cross my desk offering market direction and promises of greater returns. These prophetic propaganda pieces are from investment houses, research firms and mutual fund companies, looking to sell their services to me and then on to my clients. Sorting through the clutter each day would be impossible without a process to quickly toss away the unwanted and keep the wanted. When I say toss away, I really mean to file it in the garbage can. If I did not have a process to sort through it all, I would spend my whole day reading the tidbits of worthless information, and I would be getting nowhere. I would go down the rabbit hole and never come back out.

Investors need to be wary of the same information that they are bombarded with from the media, colleagues and family. Investors should also have a process, a quick and easy one, which allows them to toss away all of the information that is not relevant to them. In the last chapter, I talked about the promise that capital market history provides to guide us. We are rewarded in the long run for taking on short risk, to a point that the risk is actually non-existent over time. If this is true, then we need to stick to a discipline that allows for this truth to prevail and for us to prosper. Investors need a system that will allow them to stick to these truths.

The reason for the system is to help fight the good fight between your logical self and your emotional self. Most of the information you will receive, no matter its source or how good its intentions, will be a mix of statistical data mixed with a plethora of personal opinions. Each piece will be stirring within you a mix of both fear and greed. When someone you know mentions something to you, all with your best interest in mind, it will be a mix of statistical data and their personal opinion (or an opinion that they heard and accept as fact).

The statistical data is almost always short of the whole story or is not confirmed. I am not calling anyone a fabricator, but one study will lead to someone taking the data and using it to produce more statistics, and so on. After a while, the information becomes very distorted and corrupted. It is similar to when I was growing up, we used to make recordings on cassette tapes from recordings on other cassette tapes. It became full of static and other noises with each generation of duplicates.

Let's look at an example of how statistics and opinion interfere with our lives and play with our emotions. Imagine that one of your co-workers heard that the Canadian dollar fell by 2.5 cents against the US dollar, and then he proceeds to tell you that this is terrible news for the Canadian stock market. The first may be a statistical fact, but the second is not.

The Canadian dollar, moving in either direction, will always have either a negative or positive impact on something or someone else. Imagine that you leave your work after this conversation, and another talking head on the radio tells you that crude oil has jumped up in price by $2 per barrel, and then he concludes for you that this is a really good thing for the Canadian economy.

It might very well be; but it can also have negative impacts on other sectors such as transportation, manufacturing and oil-based consumables. The first comment is statistical, while the second is merely an opinion. With these two new pieces of information, which appear somewhat conflicting, you need to think rationally to see if there is some short-term change that you have to make. How can you decide? Do you need to act on this information? Are these short-term events relative to your long-term financial goals?

The media, for one, is an awesome provider of financial information. It is also a business that must sell newspapers, gain listeners or viewers or get internet traffic to their sites. The more eyes that they can get on their newspaper, TV or computer screens, the more they can sell advertising spots.

What sells more than anything else are fear and greed in relation to just about every topic in life. The newspaper, for example, has even compartmentalized what we are most emotional about: the world section, the city section, the sports section and so on. They even change the title of some of the sections to match our emotions, such as: *Your Money, Travel Today* and *Entertainment Now*.

Here is a classic exercise in order to emphasize my point. Grab a blue highlighter and a yellow highlighter from your desk drawer. Now, buy yourself a newspaper, either a local or a national one. Pick a section: world news, local news, business, money or sports. Read an article or two.

As you read the article, I want you to highlight any sentence that contains statistical data with the blue highlighter, and highlight any sentence that contains personal opinion of the writer or some source they are quoting with the yellow highlighter. After you are done with the article, count how many sentences are marked with each colour and how many sentences have not colour. Look at the ratio of blue to yellow. What do you notice?

Let me tell you a short story that happened to me way back in 1992, when I first started as a financial advisor to clients. I was working in the office one day when reception received a call from our local paper. It was a business reporter who was looking to do an article on retirement savings. The call was put through to me, not because I was the most experienced but because I was a warm body that happened to be there at the time and I had skipped lunch.

I took the call, and she asked what I was advising clients to do with their money at this time of year. I gave her a simple response that, to me, was common sense: the buy low/sell high idea of investing. At the time, I was dumbfounded that a personal finance business writer for the paper, one that I had read so often, knew very little about the basic concept of investment management.

The article came out the following week, and I was anxious to see my name quoted in the paper—and it was. What struck me, though, were two things. First, the article was written in a way that made the writer seem more expert than she truly was about the area covered. Second, it provided only clips of the conversation and the information could easily been taken out of context by the reader. I started to question everything I read in the financial media after that. I started to separate fact from fiction. I started to ignore their opinion and concentrate on facts, which made it seem as though there was very little meat left on the bone.

The next logical question to me was, "If the information in the financial media is based on misleading statistics and mere opinions, why would this not be the case in the other sections, too?"

The truth of the media is that all of this noise, all of this information and all of these providers are mere servants to their own ends. They provide commentary to a mass of readers, it can often be perceived to be advice to us as individuals and to us personally. It triggers in us very emotional responses, and we want to create rational conclusions from it. There is no rational conclusion that can come from missing facts or worse when they have been tainted with personal opinion.

So, how does one create a system or a process to cut through the clutter, in order to increase your chance of success? How can you establish a framework that allows logic to triumph over emotion?

Build your own personalized Intellectual Framework. Let your success be by design and not by a matter of coincidence.

Personal Wealth Management Strategy

An intellectual framework is a system or methodology that produces an expected long-term result.

Let's say that you have a young family and you dream of taking a trip to Disneyland, Florida, in a couple of years. The trip is a major event in your lives and one that everyone in your family dreams of. What are the basic steps that you would take to make this vacation a reality? Do you just get up and go with no thought to the trip? Of course you don't. You set some basic plans in motion. You would be answering questions such as: "When do we go? How do we get there? How much will it cost? How will we save for this? What are the risks? Are there better alternatives?" These questions must be answered at some point.

These are the intellectual things that we must deal with because we are intellectual beings. We have developed frontal lobes in our brain, and therefore require some amount of planning to help to secure our future goal.

The same is true for trying to achieve any financial goal: buying a house, retirement, educating the children or passing on wealth to the next generations. If these are the destinations we want to arrive at, we must answer some basic questions about how to get there.

The Personal Wealth Management Strategy (PWMS) is our intellectual framework. The PWMS is the umbrella under which all decision-making and outcomes are intended to dwell. A PWMS, or financial plan, asks the basic questions in a structured format. The end result is the optimized allocation of our scarce resources (time and money) to achieve our goals. Your financial plan is somewhat dynamic or changing in nature, simply because the variables and even the goals will change over time.

The PWMS has three basic planning sections and five management sections. It might sound complicated at first, but it really is simple. The three planning sections cover "what do we want", and the four management sections are about "how are we going to get there".

The three planning sections are: short-term planning, medium-term planning and long-term planning (i.e. education, boat, cottage, travel). The planning sections are macro-type views, overlooking what we want at various points in our life. Short-term planning considers things in the next 5 years. Examples of a short-term goal would be buying a home, taking a trip or paying off debt.

Medium-term planning looks at financial goals that are between 5 and 15 years. Goals for this section might include paying off a mortgage, educating the children or buying a cottage. Long-term planning is for those goals that are longer than 15 years or that transcend the medium-term planning. This generally includes things such as retirement planning and estate planning.

Once we know where we want to be in the short, medium, and long term, we next have to find a path to get there. What are the things that must be done or must occur for us to meet these goals? This is where the management sections come in.

The management sections are: cash flow management, risk management, credit management, portfolio management, and tax management. These sections are only the servants of the planning sections, as they exist and work only to achieve the goals outlined in PWMS. For some people, there might be a need to focus on one section more than another at a certain point in their personal financial lifecycle.

Cash flow management is exactly what is says. It ensures the most efficient use of cash inflows against cash outflows. The use of a family budget is a popular tool in this process. It is the tool that helps direct that income to be either spent or saved.

Risk management involves the chance of an event happening that could have a negative economic result on your goals and dreams. Is there something that can happen that will prevent us from reaching our goals? Negative events could include things such as premature death, disability, losing a job or the destruction of a personal asset.

If one of these events was to occur, what would be the impact on your future goals and dreams? If the event should happen, how would you be able to recover? The use of insurance plays a key role here, to cover the economic loss from an unwanted event. Life insurance, job loss insurance, disability insurance or home and car insurance are typical solutions.

Credit management looks at the debt that people have and how to reduce it most efficiently. Most people are aware that they should manage their investment portfolio. The goal is to get it to be large enough to provide for money-at-work, but not many people regard their debts as a portfolio. This is called your *credit portfolio*. Where investment portfolios try to grow your assets as much as possible for a given risk level, credit management aims to get your debts down as efficiently as possible and make sure you get the lowest cost, based on your credit worthiness.

Portfolio management is a main focus of this book. This area focuses on building and maintaining wealth through effective asset management. The goal is to achieve an expected and desired rate of return, within certain risk parameters and within a certain time frame. In other words, we want to grow our investment capital within our margin for potential losses by the time we need the money. We will cover this more thoroughly in the pages to come.

Tax management considers ways that we can keep more of our income in our pocket and less in the government coffers. The amount of income tax and consumption tax we pay is a major expense over a lifetime. Reducing the amount of tax that we pay is important to help to achieve our goals. Every taxpayer has an obligation to themselves to only pay their fair share of tax and not a dollar more. How this can happen is by understanding the tax laws and planning our finances to help reduce unnecessary tax.

Investment Policy Statement

With the exception of cash flow management, there are no other areas in personal finance where the 'media noise' seems to drag individuals down a path of chaos and wealth destruction.

The noise comes from an endless supply of rhetoric from pundits who have too many self-serving motives to list. There is not one investment house, financial rag or website that is truly charitable and not trying to make a dollar somehow. Now don't get me wrong. There is nothing wrong with a company profiting for a service that they provide. Consumers just need to be aware that value has a cost, and sometimes there is little value for the cost (more about that next chapter)!

In the last chapter we discussed fear and greed. We talked about how the financial industry, like many industries, has learned to market and pitch towards these motivation buttons. They scare us into buying insurance and they use our greed in order to sell us investments.

Just like having a financial plan or PWMS as an intellectual framework, so we should also have an investment plan as part of our intellectual framework. The investment plan is commonly known as the Investment Policy Statement or IPS. The IPS has been around for many years but has been a "secret weapon" of the wealthy investors, pension plans and private wealth managers. I mention the word "secret" because typical individuals do not tend to use IPS because no one ever explained it to them.

The IPS draws its strength from common sense. If you wanted to build anything successfully, you have to have a plan. If not, it becomes a hodgepodge of Band-Aids and quick fixes. You wouldn't build a house without a plan. We already established that you shouldn't build your financial future without a PWMS. I tell you now that your chance of investment success must be built on a plan or Investment Policy Statement.

So, if an IPS is so popular with the wealthy and the successful, why do we not hear about this more often? Well, to be quite frank, there are two reasons. The first reason is because it is boring and not very sexy. Imagine a newspaper article or blog that talked about long-term capital appreciation by maintaining a long-term intellectual framework. There would be nothing left to write about. The blogs and the media need to feed the frenzy with the latest, greatest and hottest ideas. To them, the topic is just too boring.

Secondly, you would not listen anyway. You would not listen because of the same reasons why the media won't talk about it. It is too boring, no matter how well it works.

So what is involved with developing an investment policy statement? That is the easy part, if you want to keep it simple. On the other hand, it can be as complex as you like. The basic idea, however, is that you are trying to create a birds-eye view of what dictates the asset allocation of an investment portfolio. In other words, we want to establish the investment goals, timeframe and expected conditions for the fulfillment of those goals.

The first consideration is *portfolio objective*, or the goal that we are trying to accomplish. We must both outline the goal and clarify the purpose. This might be a short-term goal such as saving money to cover an upcoming debt, a medium-term goal like putting aside money for a down payment on a new house or a longer-term goal such as planning your retirement income. After you have stated the goal, you must quantify the amount that you need to achieve the goal. This would be the same goal as you have stated in your PWMS.

The next consideration is the *time horizon*, which is the term for the deadline that we set to accomplish the investment result. It is the date when we need all of the money back out of our investments in order to achieve the goal we have. For example, if we want to buy a home 5 years from now, then we will need all of the investment money back for that time.

Another example would be the goal of funding the education of our children. If the child is a newborn, we might have an 18- or 20-year time horizon until we need all of the capital available.

Retirement is also a very common example of a financial goal, but it is one of which people tend to misunderstand the concept. What is the time horizon of the capital if a 50-year-old person wants to retire at 65? Most would say that the time horizon is 15 years. In truth, he might retire at 65, but I have yet to meet a retiree that needs all of his retirement accounts on the first year of retirement! Generally, the retirement assets are meant to provide an income over the next 30 years.

The time horizon is important because it lays out a timeline. In the last chapter, in capital market history, we discussed that some investments (such as ownership investments) have historically proven to outperform other types of assets (such as loanership) if the length of time is long enough. On the flip-side, some ownership investments offer too much risk if the time length is too short.

Time horizon provides a timeframe whereby the capital will be left alone to grow until it is needed. The longer the time horizon is, then the more we can let capital market history provide superior returns for our investment.

Another consideration in developing your own IPS is *required rate of return*.

The reason why we save and invest is to fulfill some financial goal or some need in the future. If this was not the case, then why would we bother at all? We might as well just spend it all. Since we are trying to save a finite amount to reach a certain financial goal by a certain future time, we must compute the final variable in the equation.

It is like taking a trip across the country. We know where we are going and we know how long it will take to get there. Now we just need to know what will be the most effective method of travel to get us there on time. We could walk, drive, take the train or fly. If we have plenty of time to spare, we could walk. If we have only a few days, we might need to fly.

The final variable is the *rate of return*, or ROR. For example, if we plan to invest $5,000 every year towards our financial goal of $500,000 in 20 years (with 20 years being our time horizon), we need to know what ROR we must achieve in order to reach our goal. In this case, the ROR is approximately 8%.

The next consideration in developing your IPS is *risk tolerance*.

Risk is a funny word. As we discussed in the previous chapter, risk means so many things to so many people. Investments have varying degrees of risk or fluctuations in value. You need to determine how much risk you are willing to accept in the short term (day-to-day or year-to-year) in order to reach your long-term goals.

When I say fluctuating values, I mean the ups and downs of the value of your investments. I can tell you this from experience: I have yet to see anyone complain about a 20% gain, but I have seen oodles of people fret over a mere 5% drop in value. Both of these are fluctuations in value. You must determine how much you can accept as a short-term loss and still remain invested.

In our story, Jakob Fuggar was adamant about following a certain principle. Regardless of the pundits and forecasters, he spread his wealth among several ships in a systematic fashion. He worked with an intellectual framework. He allowed logic to triumph over emotion.

In the next chapter, we will bring this all together in an *asset allocation strategy* that will complete your *intellectual framework*.

CHAPTER 8 ~ THE ASSET ALLOCATION METHOD

Jakob Fuggar's story

The small cottage, or *teachin*as their father liked to call it to show his Irish heritage, had the typical white-washed walls and thatched roof. In the big room downstairs, with its dusty-planked floor, there was an assortment of chairs and tables, as well as a hearth that always had a fire going. The family Bible, which seemed to be worth more than the cottage itself, sat in its own dedicated cranny off to the side of the main room.

Alexander and Elizabeth were now upstairs in their beds, separated by a half-wall on one side of the cottage. Alexander occupied the front and Elizabeth the rear. If they raised their arms, they could easily touch the slope of the thatched roof above them. Their parents' room lay on the opposite side of the cottage, complete with a door for privacy.

The warmth of the fire came up from the main floor and the smell of the extinguished beeswax candle still hung in the air.

"The smell from the beeswax is much better than when Mother burns the tallow," Elizabeth said into the darkness as she lay in her bed.

A voice replied in the darkness. "Yes, although the tallow seemed to deaden the smell of the over-cooked mutton," Alexander whispered, hoping Mother did not hear him.

"What do you think that Herr Fuggar was talking about when he said, 'Not all my wealth is in one place'?" Elizabeth asks her brother. It was obvious that she, too, was thinking about the conversation that took place that morning at the merchant office.

"I think Herr Fuggar was talking about his gold not being in one location, but that is my best guess," Alexander replied. "I wager that he has too much gold to hold in any one place anyway, as it would surely fill this cottage alone."

"Maybe he is just afraid that a thief would steal it if he leaves it in one place," Elizabeth added to the conversation.

The next morning, as they walked up the slippery morning cobble walk to the front door of their employment, Alexander pointed out the four-coloured cornerstone.

"See, I told you that its four distinct hues all seem to blend perfectly together in the middle," Alexander explained as he opened the door to let his sister pass inside first.

"Good morning, Herr Fuggar," Elizabeth said with her brilliant smile.

As expected, Jakob Fuggar was sitting at his desk with his head bent down, staring at the papers in front of him. His concentration was broken by Elizabeth's entry. It was like a ray of sunshine was cast directly into his eyes as he squinted back to the siblings.

"Aye, you're just in time. The carracks were unloaded yesterday, and now we will spend today preparing them for their return sail," Jakob replied like a trumpet. Obviously the unloaded haul from yesterday was a financial success, as Herr Fuggar had an extra jump in his unusual gait. There was a reason that he was known as *Fuggar the Rich*.

Having removed their overcoats and brushed off their boots, Alexander and Elizabeth stood in front of the employer's desk, awaiting any special orders for the day.

"Miss Elizabeth, you need to ask the town merchants to re-supply the stores aboard ship for the crew," Jakob demanded. He handed her a written letter of instruction to show the various merchants, such as the baker, the butcher and the candlestick maker.

"Boy, you need to visit Jack the Scot about the supply of whisky to be sent to those ninnies in England. Also, boy, you need to speak to Brother Kelly at the priory about the two priests who will be going to France aboard the boats," Herr Fuggar ordered in a commanding tone.

"Sir, what would you have me do with the two priests? Do I put one on each ship as you explained yesterday?" Alexander asked with a smile, feeling quite proud of his wit.

"You are a funny lad, Alexander!" Jakob laughed at the thought of telling Brother Kelly he was going to split up the pair of priests between two ships in order to be safe. "No need for that, boy. Surely, my casks that are filled with a different holy spirit will sink, but I am sure that the men of God will cling to their wooden crosses and will float safely." Jakob replied with a smile at his own wit.

"Sir, may I be so bold as to ask you to explain why you said 'Not all my wealth is in one place' yesterday?" Elizabeth asked, after Herr Fuggar had a chance to relish in his own comedy.

Jakob the Rich sat back down in his chair, cupping and stroking his grey beard in his right hand.

"Miss Elizabeth, why do you think I feel the need to keep my wealth in different places?" Jakob asked her.

"Well, my brother and I think that it is because you have too much gold to hold in one cottage," Elizabeth replied.

"I think that it is because you are afraid of thieves," Alexander added, not wanting to be part of Elizabeth's theory.

"It is true that I have much wealth, and it is true-have no doubt-that I do not want to be visited by a thief in the night either," Jakob agreed. "As certain as I am about my wealth, I am also certain that there are many great houses, even here in Ireland, that can easily store my gold . . . if I had all of my money in gold."

Herr Fuggar continued, "What good would it do me to let my gold sit idle inside King John's Castle? If this was my intent, then I invite to dinner the very thief that I prefer to avoid!"

Elizabeth and Alexander both were confused. What thief could scale the stone walls and get past the King's sentry?

"A gold piece that is not handled will lose its brilliant shine. In the same way, a three-crown piece tomorrow might not buy the same dram of whisky as a three-crown piece today. The coin would be worth less. In the same way, what good is it for a shepherd to keep his rams from his ewes? Would his flock not diminish over time? Would he not be better to let the flock multiply?" Herr Fuggar queried.

The brother and sister looked at each other and then back at the old man behind the desk.

Alexander asked, "Well, we can't put two sovereigns to pasture and hope for a lamb in the Spring? How would you suggest that we keep our gold from becoming idle?"

"You put it to work, much the same as what you should be doing for me right now!" Jakob Fuggar laughed out loud again at his own wit. Alexander and Elizabeth were not sharing in the irony.

"Much of man's wealth should be put to work and not sit idle," Jakob Fuggar explained. "The problem before you is this: with what should we entrust our wealth? Do we lend it, become a merchant of trade, become a landowner or hold gold for safety?"

"There is but one single, correct answer to this problem. Truly, the wise man understands that wealth should be spread among each of these options equally. When things are going well, business will do well, and your lending and business ventures will be profitable. So, too, will a landowner profit during most seasons. When the times become tough during war or drought, wealth held in gold will be a wise choice."

Jacob Fuggar stood up and walked over to the window. The sun was up, and there was a slight fog on the quay.

Alexander and Elizabeth joined him at the window. Herr Fuggar looked upon the quay with his three ships sitting tall in the harbour.

"As I do not put all of my valuable goods upon one ship, I don't put all of my wealth in one area. A man who entrusts all his wealth to one boat will be no more profitable than by spreading the wealth. To do so comes with much unwarranted risk, and it therefore is the folly of fools," Herr Fuggar said as he turned and faced them.

"So, should wealth be cast among these four and then forgotten?" Elizabeth asked. "Surely, we must keep a watchful eye on each of these vessels, because our wealth is in their keep?"

"Miss Elizabeth, you are as keen a learner as your brother!" Jakob replied. "Only a fool would cast their seed upon fertile soil and not water and tend to the weeding of the garden. Over time, each venture will have their moment in God's sunshine. If you allocate your wealth evenly among these four concerns, you will never find them to remain equal. A wise man takes the excess profits from one of the ventures and re-allocates them to the venture that have not done so well."

Alexander was excited to have learned a lesson that would provide food for his thoughts all day. "Herr Fuggar, is this the secret to how you have amassed such wealth?"

"Aye, Alexander, my boy. You are a bold one. True, you are. This is one of the great secrets to my wealth. Every great building is built upon a solid cornerstone, and this is my cornerstone." Jakob concluded as he waved the two of them back to work.

Jacob Fuggar, commonly known as Fuggar the Rich, was a German merchant and banker who lived in the 1500's. Although he may never have visited the shores of Ireland or employed a young Alexander and Elizabeth, he is credited with the comment that wealth should be divided equally into four sections: stocks, bonds, real estate and gold.

The concept of dividing wealth is not new. It has been around since the beginning of time, as most common sense approaches have. You can also find the concept within Shakespeare's "Merchant of Venice", when the merchant Antonio says to his friend Solanio:

> *My ventures are not in one bottom trusted,*
> *Nor to one place; nor is my whole estate*
> *Upon the fortune of this present year:*
> *Therefore my merchandise makes me not sad.*

This idea of dividing wealth is most commonly known today as *asset allocation*. Asset allocation puts into play the strategy of Jakob Fuggar and Shakespeare's Merchant. For example, Herr Fuggar explained to the young brother and sister that gold should not be left to tarnish in the keep of the castle but rather putting it to work. In this, he is explaining that wealth needs to be invested. He then continues with the idea that, once invested, it must not be all upon one ship at sea. Shakespeare's Antonio agrees.

What makes the strategy of asset allocation so strong is that it first leads investors to diversify their wealth among different assets. Then, it forces our thoughts into which types of assets and the benefits of each.

Before we talk about how to allocate our assets, let us begin with a short discussion on what diversification is and how we can diversify our investments.

Diversification

The basic concept of diversification is to reduce the overall risk to an investment portfolio without reducing the return. This is done by marrying together various holdings or investments to create a more certain outcome with an expected degree of risk (i.e. value variability).

Modern Portfolio Theory (MPT), which can be quite involved and complex, looks at the relationship of diversification as a means to reduce risk without limiting returns. William Sharpe is credited as the father of MPT back in the 1960's. Part of his findings consisted of historical evidence, showing that there are some risks that you can avoid and some that you must accept. Although I will not go into the whole concept of MPT, I will share the two risks he outlines: *systematic risk* and *unsystematic risk*.

Systematic risk, also known as market risk, is the risk that is contained within the specific market that you are investing in. For example, let's say you bought a house in a small industrial city that had one or two large employers, such as a paper mill or an auto manufacturing plant. If the employer is doing really well, the wages are steady and it employs much of the local workforce, then the chances are that there will be many people in a position to buy a house. The general real estate market in that town will most likely rise if supply is slower than the demand for houses. If the opposite occurs and there is a slowdown in the industrial employer, which creates layoffs, then the chances are that the supply of housing will become greater than the demand, and you will ultimately see house values fall. The change in the house values will be partly reflected by the real estate market for that small city in general.

This is very much like Herr Fuggar's ships, sitting at the Limerick Quay. Each ship is its own vessel, just like each house is its own domain. However, as the tide rises and falls, so must all the ships in the harbour rise and fall--none more or less than the others.

Therefore, systematic risk is a risk that you cannot avoid. It is the risk that you must assume when you choose to buy a house. It is the same risk that you assume when you invest in any asset. If you buy shares in a company that trades on a stock market, the value placed on the stock at any given time will be partly determined by the sentiment of the general market.

Unsystematic risk, or *asset-specific risk*, is the second type of risk that investors need to be aware of. This risk exists, not because of the market, but because of the actual investment itself. It is the risk in that particular asset and not the asset class. All the boats in the harbour may rise and fall with the tide, so long as they have a hull. If one specific boat has a rotten hull, the tide may rise in the harbour, but the boat will surely flounder and sink in the rising tide.

In the example of the house in the industrial city, the economy might be booming, and there might be a strong demand for housing, but one particular house may have problems that make it almost impossible to sell. At least, it may not sell at the market rate. The house could have mold, rotten foundation, contaminated land or a whole list of other factors specific to that house. The same is true if we invest in shares of a business. The market, or even the sector of the economy, might be strong, but the company might have some serious problems of its own.

These two risks are important to understand as investors, simply because of this: one risk we WANT to accept, and the other we WANT to avoid.

Systematic risk is unavoidable. We invest in a certain market or asset class because we want to achieve the long-term results (as we discussed in the previous chapter). -We want to achieve our financial goals, and we use various assets because they provide returns relative to their risk (market risk).

With Systematic risk, there is no way to avoid it. You cannot remove or even reduce the risk associated with a market. If you buy one stock or one house, you will be affected by the general market ebbs and flows.

Unsystematic risk is avoidable. We invest in a market to achieve returns that are historically characteristic with that market. We cannot outperform a market over the long term. We can, however, accept the return that the market provides and we attempt with prudence to limit risk and cost in doing so. The problem lies not in getting the market return as much as assuming too much risk in using this strategy.

If there is a risk associated with owning one house in a real estate market, or owning one stock in the stock market, then the easiest way to reduce that risk is NOT to own just one house or one stock. Jakob Fuggar in our fictional story said this: *"As I do not put all of my valuable goods upon one ship, I don't put all my wealth in one area. A man who entrusts all his wealth to one boat will be no more profitable than by spreading the wealth. To do so comes with much unwarranted risk, and it is therefore the folly of fools".*

In short, you are rewarded for taking on market risk, but you get no extra reward for taking on asset-specific risk. Therefore, you must try to eliminate the latter form of risk by casting your wealth among various assets. This is what diversification seeks to accomplish.

There is an old saying in the investment community: *"God knows everything. The rest of us must diversify."*

How to diversify

The idea of spreading our wealth is simple in theory. In practice, it becomes a little more complex.

Simply casting wealth across different investments may not accomplish as much as one would think—if it is not done with some thoughtful planning. If you want to remove the risk of owning stocks in the stock market, but all you buy is two or three of the big banks, you may not be truly reducing risk. I call this "di-worse-ification".

Diversification can be done in several ways, but here are a few of the most common that people should think about:

Asset type - Spread the wealth between stocks, bonds, cash/gold, and real estate.

Asset Quality - Spread your wealth among large and small companies or various credit worthiness bonds.

Geographically - Spread your wealth among the different economies of the world and political backdrops.

Maturity - Spread your wealth among different maturity of investments over time.

Business Cycle Sensitivity - Spread your wealth between companies that react differently in periods of the economic cycle.

Interest Rate Sensitivity - Spread your wealth among assets that react differently to changes in interest rates

Currency - Spread your wealth among difference currencies to reduce currency risk

Style - Spread your wealth among different money manager styles (Value, Growth, and Momentum).

These various methods of diversification are important tools that can greatly reduce the risk in an investor's portfolio. An individual who chooses not to take advantage of them is foolish.

Sometimes, we choose not to diversify because we feel it might actually be more risky. This is generally a result of ignorance. Let me give you a great example of how crazy we can be when it comes to keeping to a known comfort.

I was born in and currently live in Canada. I am truly proud of my country, just like the rest of the Canadians around me. I am sure, wherever you live and call home, you are proud of it, too. Over the past 25 years of working with Canadian clients and their investment portfolios, I have come to realize that most people tend to hold the vast majority, if not all of it, in Canadian investments. How much of your own portfolio is held in Canadian-based assets?

I have been amazed, in my many years as a wealth advisor, when I get to discuss investing with people at kitchen tables, coffee shops, pubs or at my office. When I meet with someone and I observe that they have all of their investments in Canada, they typically tell me that it is safe. They feel that it is safer than investing overseas. I ask them why they feel that way, and they don't really have an answer, other than that it seemed like the safe thing to do.

To stoke the conversation further, I would put forth a quick question. I ask them to choose one of the following countries, other than Canada, to invest their portfolio in: Italy, China, the UK, France or Japan. They usually only choose one of those countries. Typically, when I ask this, the client looks at me as if I am crazy.

This is usually followed up with a second question for them: "If we were sitting in Italy right now, enjoying a bottle of Chianti with some antipasto, or we were sharing a bottle of Bordeaux and a baguette in France, or we were sucking on Sushi with a cup of Saki in Japan, would the conversation be different? What if we were sitting there with that being our home country, and I told you to invest 100% of your wealth in Canada? You would think I was nuts! Why Canada?!?

This example shows that most investors falsely assume that their own country is the best place to invest their money.

The strangest part of this subject is that each of the countries mentioned have both a larger stock exchange and a larger *gross domestic product* than Canada does. Canada recently ranked number 9 and number 10 respectively in the world, well behind those other markets.

As I had mentioned in a previous chapter, risk is generally associated with both our experience and our understanding of the potential outcomes. The key here is to diversify. Sometimes, what might seem riskier on its own may very well be less risky when combined with other holdings.

Strategic asset allocation

The question is not whether we should allocate assets, but rather how we are to do it effectively. How do we match up a target risk and target return with what we are trying to accomplish?

If we follow the intellectual framework of the IPS, then we have the answer already starting to come to light. In the process of producing your personalized Investment Policy Statement, you determine what you would like to achieve, over what period of time and with which level of risk. The next step is to allocate assets to match those goals.

For the sake of simplicity in this book, we will break the decision into three basic parts:

- safety
- income
- growth and appreciation

These three parts are key factors in determining how much capital we should have in low-risk shorter-term investments vs high-return longer-term investments. The various mixes will produce different return and risk characteristics.

The more we place in growth and appreciation-type investments, then the greater the long-term return potential and also the greater the short-term risk. On the other hand, the more capital that we place in low-risk shorter-term investments will produce a risk and lower long-term return.

What is appropriate for you is determined on an individual basis.

In some text books, there is a concept more commonly known as the "100 minus your age" rule. It simply suggests that as your age increases, so should the percentage you have in safer, short-term investments. Someone who is 40-years-old should have 60% of their wealth in growth investments and 40% in safe, income-producing assets.

Someone who is 25-years-old should have 75% in growth. An 80-year-old should have only 20% in growth-oriented holdings. As a rule of thumb, it seems to work, and it works particularly well when trying to explain the basic concept of asset allocation. The truth is, the actual amount to be held in either of these two distinct areas is determined by many factors, with age only being one of those factors.

There are six basic allocations that most investors' portfolios will tend to look like, based on the criteria in their Investment Policy Statement:

- Capital Preservation Portfolio,
- Income Portfolio,
- Conservative Portfolio,
- Balanced Portfolio,
- Growth Portfolio, and
- Aggressive Growth Portfolio.

Each of these basic portfolio allocations have a certain risk and return feature that will fit with most clients' investment needs and objectives. Let us take a quick look at each of these. I have put into brackets the general percentage between cash/bonds/stocks in order to help you to understand the allocation.

- **Capital Preservation Portfolio (100/0/0)**

Investors who are looking to secure the short-term value of their investment with very little risk will look to this portfolio. The make-up of this portfolio will be 100% invested in short-term Government of Canada Bonds, T-bills or other short-term money market investments.

The return on these investments will reflect the lack of risk, and investors should expect little, if any, return. The total return of this portfolio will be from interest with virtually no capital appreciation.

You must remember that an asset can also depreciate and create losses, which does not keep within the needed framework of safety of capital. The time horizon for capital in the capital preservation portfolio is under 2 years.

- **Income Portfolio (0/100/0)**

As the name suggests, this portfolio allocation will provide a high interest-based cash flow with low degree of risk. The holdings in this type of portfolio will be made up almost entirely of fixed income investments, such as Government of Canada bonds, foreign sovereign bonds and domestic or foreign corporate bonds. Some income portfolios may include a small amount towards high-yielding dividend payers, such as banks and utility companies. The time horizon for this portfolio should be at least 2 years.

- **Conservative Portfolio (0/70/30)**

Many investors need some growth in their portfolios to help offset the effects of inflation over time. Balancing a portfolio with some growth-oriented investments can help to achieve this. If an investor is somewhat risk-adverse but requires some capital appreciation over time, the Conservative Portfolio will fit their need. The basic time horizon is at least 3 years.

- **Balanced Portfolio (0/50/50)**

If an investor is trying to achieve a mix of income needs (or safety of principle) and the potential risk of growth investments, the Balanced Portfolio is a fine choice. The balance between each of these areas provides the best of both worlds, resulting in a combination of moderate capital appreciation, interest income and medium level of risk. The time horizon needed for this type of portfolio should be 5 years or greater.

- **Growth Portfolio (0/30/70)**

For investors who are looking to reduce the risk associated with having all their investments in growth-oriented investments, the smaller holdings in bonds will reduce the fluctuations in the portfolio value. As most of the holdings are in equity or stock holdings, the expected return for this portfolio is higher, but so is the overall risk in any given year. The time horizon for a growth portfolio investor should be at least one business cycle of 5 to 10 years or more.

- **Aggressive Growth Portfolio (0/0/100)**

This is riskiest of the asset-allocated portfolios. The main theme of this type of portfolio is to maximize long-term growth by investing only in equity or stock investments. By holding only shares in quality businesses, the return expectation is the highest, and therefore the resulting risk level is also the highest in the short term. The time horizon for this type of portfolio should be at least 1 to 2 economic cycles, which is at least 10 to 15 years.

These 6 structured portfolios, which set the initial allocation, are known as Strategic Asset Allocations. These are the templates that your funding will flow into. It is the intellectual framework of your investments that will lead to a more results-based approach to investing and less of performance-based or cost-based investing (as we will see in the next chapter).

Dynamic asset allocation

Of course, like with all things, change is inevitable. At the beginning of the year, you might have determined by your intellectual framework that you are a Balanced Portfolio investor, and you may have made investments where 50% of your holdings were in bonds and 50% were in stocks. That was then, but this is now the end of the year, and the portfolio is not 50/50 anymore.

Things change. Stocks go up. Stocks go down. Bonds go up. Bonds go down. You might find that, at the end of a year, your stock portfolio rose 10% and your bonds rose only 2%. You are worth more because your overall portfolio did well, but now you find that you are "over-weighted" in stocks because of their growth.

Imagine that your Investment Policy Statement (your intellectual framework for investments) dictates that you maintain a 50% weighting in each of these two areas. You must, by virtue of your IPS, re-balance your investment account back to 50/50 when it falls offside and one area is larger than the other. By doing this, you are making two important moves. First, you are maintaining the level of risk that you want by keeping the growth investments down to the level they should be. Secondly, when you sell the higher-performing asset, you are (in theory) selling high and buying low. It is a fairly common sense activity.

As part of your Investment Policy Statement (IPS), you should include a summary of under what circumstances and at what time you will automatically adjust your portfolio. If you do not have it written in your IPS, the chance of failing to re-allocate becomes great. This is because we are back to trying to second-guess a market, and this is based mostly on emotions and not logic.

The asset allocation methods discussed in this chapter are based on the use of an Investment Policy Statement that targets a certain risk level and a certain return expectation. It is by planning and continuous monitoring that we can effectively reduce risk to expected levels with diversification. It is with planning that we can craft a portfolio that will produce a certain long-term return. It is with this intellectual framework we can allow logic to triumph over emotion.

Many years ago, the wise Jakob Fuggar the Rich stated that a man should divide his wealth and maintain that framework. Those lessons still apply today.

CHAPTER 9 ~ PRICE AND VALUE

Dee and Sharon's story

The snap from the opening footrest startled the cat, which had just nestled down on the couch opposite the recliner chair. In the background, the sound of the dishwasher had just started with the gentle sound of spraying water against plates and cutlery. The sound was much like a pulsating lawn sprinkler.

Supper had ended, and with everything put away and cleaned up, Dee found himself relaxing a few minutes earlier than usual on a quiet Friday night. The only thing missing, he thought, was the evening *Freeholder*. The *Freeholder* was the local newspaper, and it generally arrived around 6pm each Friday—which was still another 15 minutes away. Dee hoped that the delivery boy had finished his supper early and would be around a little sooner.

The Friday night *Freeholder* was an important part of his week. The only sections that he cared about were a few editorials, the weekly crossword and the dozens of flyers that came with it. His wife Sharon would join him shortly. Together, they liked the quiet Friday nights after supper. Unlike Dee, she liked other sections, such as Entertainment and the City section.

What they did share was the joy of looking up the great deals that could be had that week at the local stores. They never thought of themselves as bargain hunters or coupon-clippers, but they were. They might not know the price of everything, but they surely knew the value. This is the bargain hunter's greatest skill.

Every week, the centre of the *Freeholder* was overloaded with offers and coupons from virtually every store imaginable. Promotional flyers from clothing stores, groceries chains, electronics outlets, flower boutiques and the plumbing store all came together in one mess of a paper.

A cry came from the back room where Sharon had gone to get her slippers. "Did you check to see if Jimmy dropped off the paper yet, Dee?"

"No, not yet. I hope Jimmy doesn't forget about us again," Dee replied. They had the same paperboy for the past 3 years, and little Jimmy never did miss their house, except for one time during the coldest day last winter. The snow was blowing, and, for whatever reason, Jimmy walked right past their house.

"Dee, little Jimmy never misses our house!" Sharon said excitedly as she emerged from the back room with her slippers and housecoat on.

Just as she entered the living room, both of them heard the familiar creak from the mailbox outside. Jimmy had come early. They both looked at each other and then gave a little smile.

Sharon went to the front door to retrieve the newspaper. By the time that she had opened the door and stepped out, little Jimmy was already two doors down the street.

"Well, come on in and let's have a look at the week's specials," Dee said, not having moved an inch from the comfort of his blue recliner. He was leaned back slightly in the chair with his feet up on the footrest. He was a king in his castle for sure, he thought. The reading lamp beside him was on and ready for action.

"I'm coming. Hold your horses, mister!" Sharon replied as she re-entered the living room with the newspaper folded in two. The multitude of flyers was sticking out everywhere, threatening to spill onto the floor.

Sharon carefully passed the sections to Dee that he most wanted, along with a few of his favourite store flyers. She then took the sections that she wanted, along with various flyers that had caught her attention.

For Dee, there was one flyer that stood out among them all. This one flyer carried the best deals and savings; it was from a local hardware store that also specialized in sports equipment, auto supplies and garden tools. The retailer was a multi-department store, and the large red triangle on the front of the flyer gave it away each week.

Sharon was careful to keep the flyers she wanted, and knew that Dee didn't care for them. The flyers that she liked best were the women's clothing store and the offers from various grocery stores.

Dee snapped the flyers in mid-air to open them, as if he was cracking a whip. "There is a set of ratchets on sale this week," Dee announced. "Pretty good price . . . 60% off tomorrow only and a limited supply. I had better get to the store early."

"Do you need another set? I bought you a set last Christmas. You know, the set with the red case," Sharon pointed out, knowing he wasn't really listening. "I think it is downstairs in the laundry room."

"Yes, I know," he grunted back. He not only had a set of ratchets in a red case down stairs, but he also had a set in the back shed with a black case. "I am picking up a set for Allen, because he needs a set." Allen was their son, who had recently married. "You can't argue with the price!" Dee rationalized.

Sharon wasn't ignoring him completely, but she did not respond. This was typical Friday evening chatter. She had her own flyers to contend with, let alone his.

As Sharon flipped through the pages of the women's clothing flyer, she found nothing of any interest. Once the flyer was read, she moved on to the next one.

"Wow, stop the bus!" she cried out. Dee looked up at her over his reading glasses. "Kettleman's has canned tuna on sale for a dollar a can. The sale is for tomorrow morning only, and the limit is 6 per person! That is a bargain. A dollar a can is an unheard of price in the history of canned tuna! These cans are usually about two dollars. What a steal!"

Dee knew what that meant. He would be going to the grocery store in the morning to act as her mule. She could only buy 6 cans, and he would need to be the second person in order to get the 12 cans that she wanted. If Allen was still living at home, he would be a mule, too.

"I need to get to those ratchets first thing tomorrow, before they are gone, Sharon." Dee pleaded that his ratchet case was more important than her tuna cans, but he knew it would be a losing battle.

"You can get Allen's ratchets after the grocery store. It will only take a few minutes to run in and get six cans each," Sharon explained with a matriarchal tone.

"Yes, dear," Dee mumbled as he turned his head and started to read the business section of the newspaper. Sharon looked over as he pulled the paper up. Dee's face was replaced by the main headline, "Markets Head Lower... Stocks at All Time Lows!"

The cat jumped back onto the couch and curled at Sharon's feet, as she returned back to her sections of the newspaper. The dishwasher had stopped. There was a quiet in the house with only an occasional sound of the newspaper shuffling.

———

Lord Darlington: What cynics you fellows are!

Cecil Graham: What is a cynic?

Lord Darlington: A man who knows the price of everything and the value of nothing.

Cecil Graham: And a sentimentalist, my dear Darlington, is a man who sees an absurd value in everything, and doesn't know the market price of any single thing!"

- *"Lady Windermere's Fan", by Oscar Wilde*

In that quote, Cecil mentioned the price of something and the value of something. Any one thing can simultaneously have both price and value. It doesn't matter what it is: a house, a car, a piece of art or even shares in a business. These two things have such different meanings and are often confused.

When it comes to our daily lives, we often have to make decisions about price and value. Anytime we visit a store, we look at the price and we compare it to the value. It is no different than what Sharon and Dee did in the story.

The old saying, "A fool and his money are soon parted," is true only because they foolishly ignore value for the price they pay for something. Thankfully, most people do not think this way very often.

When you purchased this book, or even when you decided to read it, you had to come to a conclusion that the value was greater or equal to the price. The cost to buy the book would have to be fair value for the benefit you expected to receive from it. In that case the time necessary to read the book would be time well spent. This, I believe, is what has led you all the way into Chapter Nine.

PRICE AND VALUE

A few years ago, my wife and I were cleaning out the remaining items from my mother-in-law's house. She had moved into a retirement home, and in order to sell the home, we needed to downsize and remove years of items that had built up over time. It was not an easy job. The physical labour was not the issue, but it was more the decision of what to do with all the things that carried such sentimental feelings to the family.

Keeping the contents of the home was not a rational option, but pitching it to the curb was unthinkable. The family grappled with almost every item. What had value? If it could be sold, what should the price be? It was a horrible experience, even though the family did quite well working together, considering the emotional stress of the situation. This is a common occurrence for many families as our society experiences aging parents and downsizing homes.

The difference between price and value became very clear during the house clean up.

Did you ever try to clean out your own closet? Did you ever try to get rid of something that does not fit or is worn out? It is difficult to toss things away because we believe that they have value still. Other people wouldn't give you 5 cents for the item that you believe to be worth much more. It is because it is worth much more to you and you alone.

The price of something is generally viewed from the point of view of the seller, whereas the cost is the amount from the purchaser's vantage point. The price is set as a hopeful or desired amount the seller wishes to achieve, and it is based on their perception of value. Sometimes these numbers do not align so well when the buyer and the seller view a particular item.

While cleaning out the house, we gathered a number of china mugs, figurines and curiosities that my mother-in-law had amassed. In some way, this was a continuation of a habit that was formed generations ago during the Victorian period. In those days, shelves were filled with collectibles such as china cups, spoons, tiny bells, thimbles, porcelain figures, silver serving sets and other such oddities.

Over time, and as generations passed, the desire to have these collectibles has become less. Today, very few people (outside of collectors) have their home decorated with these trinkets like their grandparents or great-grandparents did. Neither is wrong or right. It is what it is. The value of most of these items, apart from the occasional rarity, was lost in the generational change.

As consumers, we look to determine the value of something, and then we compare the price that is being asked. If the price is unreasonable in comparison to our perception of value, then we may simply walk away. If the price is fair or below what we believe to be its value, then we may have a reason to trade.

How would you like to buy my car for $5,000?

Strange question, I know, since I am not selling it right now, but let's pretend that I am. Are you interested in buying it? I will even toss in a full tank of gas worth about $50. Are you interested?

What went through your mind when I asked this? Did you think about the $5,000 amount or did you wonder what kind of car I was selling? Did you picture a car worth much more or a car worth much less?

It is an interesting exercise. I ask many students that I teach or groups that I speak to this same question, and, for the most part, they all look at me with a stunned expression on their faces. The reason is because I asked a price for something, but I had left out the main component: the ability for them to perceive the item's value. Unless you are the fool that is soon parted from his money, you must be able to place a value on the item that you are considering.

In our story above, Sharon knew the usual price of a can of tuna, and she established its value in her mind as $2 per can. When she saw the offering price of $1, she was able to determine that this was a great deal. Dee, on the other hand, might not have known the price before the discount, but he certainly saw the discount—which framed his mind around the great deal to be had.

When we are consumers of *durable goods*, we choose to buy them at a price that is fair or better. This is very much like the "buy low" half of the investment strategy of "buy low, sell high". The difference with durable goods is that we don't end up selling anything afterwards, but we consume it instead.

When it comes to making investment decisions, we look to the whole common sense strategy of "buy low, sell high". This, however, has its challenges, as I had mentioned in previous chapters with respect to emotion and logic.

Let me change the story of Dee and Sharon a little bit. Let us pretend, instead of them looking at a grocery store flyer, that Sharon was looking at a flyer from an investment firm. Perhaps the firm placed a flyer into the *Freeholder* with all the other flyers. It was a colourful and attractive flyer, similar to the others in the scattering of flyers. This promotional flyer had on its front page a selection of items that were boldly announced as 20%, 40% and even 75% off the previously listed price.

Instead of the items being cans of tuna, socket sets or women's clothing, they were shares in quality companies. The investment flyer contained captions such as, "Last week $100 per share, this week $60 per share", "Today only--25% off yesterday's price", "Limited time offer" or "Quantities may be limited".

With the socket set and the cans of tuna, Sharon and Dee were ready to give up their Saturday morning and to go there when the stores opened in order to get their deals.

Do you think that many people would be lining up at the investment firm's office to pick up these hot deals in a similar way? I can tell you this: absolutely not. All you would hear and see outside their doors is crickets chirping and tumbleweeds passing in the parking lot.

If a firm was crazy enough to do this, the comments would be more along these lines: "I am not going to buy something that has gone down in price; I don't care what the value is! Are you crazy?"

Instead, Dee and many other people will run out to buy a socket set that they don't even need, just because the price is too good to give up. Sharon will load up with as much tuna as possible, given the great deal on tuna. They would not think of the investment offers in the same way. Even worse, the socket set is guaranteed to become worthless over time and a can of tuna will eventually return to the sea.

As a matter of fact, this is so true that investment firms often do the opposite of what they should be doing. Instead of promoting "buy low, sell high" offers, they often produce marketing material that promotes products that have done extremely well. Instead of the discount price of a company's share being displayed, you get to see the amazing returns other people would have made.

This is not your return, but someone else's! This promotional activity is a disservice to investors, and it distorts what is considered a prudent investment philosophy. It is equivalent of the grocery store telling people that the $2 can of tuna is now 30% more at the new price of $2.60!

Do you see the craziness in this? In the case of tuna and socket wrenches, we have an adherence to the idea of "buy low" driven by *price vs value*. It seems logical. On the other hand, when it comes to investments, there is trepidation to do the same. Trepidation (or the fear of something bad happening) is an emotional response, not a logical one.

As the net accumulators of wealth that most of us are (hence the reason you are reading this book), think about this for a moment. It would seem logical that if a quality company had a drop in the price of its shares, we should be grabbing as much as we can. If it is a six can limit, so be it. Give me six cans!

What do you do when faced with investments that have dropped in price? How do you feel?

The battle of logic over emotions continues on.

The reason for so much trepidation and fear is not because we are incapable of making logical decisions. It is more so because we have no sense of an item's value. In the absence of value, any price is irrelevant to the conversation. In the presence of determined value, price becomes easy to understand. Remember that price and value are not the same. If the investment firm were to publish the "value" of the quality company, it may make some difference to us as it gives some point of reference.

At the end of one my classes not too long ago, a student (who I will call Kevin) came up and asked me if a particular stock was a "good buy". The question was timely, because this particular stock had fallen 10% that afternoon. Kevin was one of the better finance students in the class and had a good deal of common sense about him. The conversation went something like this:

"Sir, do you have a minute?" Kevin asked me.

"Absolutely, Kevin. What's up?" I replied as I gathered my papers.

"I am not sure if you are aware, but *Pear Computer* fell by 10% today on the stock market. I was wondering if this was a good time to buy shares in it."

"I guess that would depend on what you thought it was worth?" I responded.

"The price is $82 per share," Kevin said with a certain confidence in his voice.

"Ok, what is it worth, Kevin?" I asked.

"It's worth $82 per share. That is the latest closing price," Kevin reiterated.

"Ok, but what is it worth, Kevin?" I asked again, knowing that it would frustrate Kevin a little bit.

"I checked before coming up here, and it has $82/share. That was the latest price that it traded at on the market," Kevin said with a little annoyance in his voice.

"Oh, I see. Did you want to buy my car for $5,000?" I asked.

Kevin smiled and our conversation quickly turned to baseball.

The conversation with Kevin was simple. He mistakenly confused *price* and *value*. There was no way to answer Kevin's question rationally without a determination of the value of Pear Computer. Kevin realized this, as he had already been tormented by my lecture on price and value. He, and his classmates, had already been asked if they wanted to buy my car.

Intrinsic value

There are various methods of portfolio management that drive portfolio managers on the decision whether to buy or sell any investment. It is the opinion of this author that the greatest ally to investors is this: buy companies, or any investment for that matter, when they are below what they are truly worth. In other words, buy one dollar for 50 cents.

Some people have a problem with this concept at first because there is a risk that the price is low because the investment is bad. The value of a business or a stock might be falling because the company is failing. This may be true, but once again, we are not talking about the true value (which is how you calculate what the price should be) versus what the price currently is. As Warren Buffet has been quoted as saying, *"Price is what you pay. Value is what you get."* There are plenty of assets that have a price lower than what it once was and for good reason. It is the value that is lower.

When we talk about buying $1 for 50cents, we are truly talking about buying something that we believe to be worth $1 for a price of 50cents. For Sharon, it was a $2 can of tuna for only $1. With investments, if we build a portfolio around assets that were acquired below their true value, we will see the market eventually reward us as it realizes the mispricing.

The concept seems pretty simple. It just means that you should never over-pay for something--you should under-pay for the item. When we take this approach, we automatically benefit from an investment management concept called *margin safety*. If we can find an asset that trades below its true value, it is far less likely that the price will fall further from the true value. This is compared to assets where the price is in excess of the true value or *intrinsic value*.

Intrinsic value, also known as *fundamental value*, is the true underlying value of an asset, which includes all tangible and intangible aspects. It is the anchor to which price can be compared. It exists, and it can be determined for all financial assets and real assets, such as stocks, bonds, real estate, foreign currency and other assets.

The act of buying assets at a discount to value, or using "buy low, sell high", does not always work. It fails when we value an asset wrongly. This can occur, and it certainly will occur at times. To reduce the chance of this misfortunate event occurring, we must learn as much about the asset as possible and continue to monitor the valuation. Company valuations, although not as volatile as price, are dynamic, and they change as the variables in the calculation changes.

How do you determine *intrinsic value*? Well, that conversation requires a whole new book!

For the sake of our investment discussion here, we will consider a couple of simple concepts.

What is the value of a business that has no business? In other words, what is the long-term value of a business that has no cash flow or is consistently losing money? I would hope that you would agree that the answer is: no value at all. If a company was losing money each year, there is little value except the immediate salvage value of the assets it owns, such as equipment and supplies. Over time, these assets will depreciate to zero, ultimately leaving a business that is laid to waste and ruin. It is an empty, deserted shell. Imagine an Old West ghost town with tumble weeds in the foreground and the sound of crickets in the background!

From this, we can argue that only a business that has a sustainable operation has value. If the business is to have value, it needs to be doing more than just surviving. It must have positive cash flow.

The value of a business is therefore more than just the breakup value or book value. It is, more importantly, a function of the cash flows or revenues that the business will create in the future. With this, we can say that the business value today must take into account all of these future cash flows. The greater the future cash flows, the greater the current value.

The worth of a business can be determined as the lump sum value today that is equal to a series of cash flow payments over a future period of time.

The lump sum amount of worth today is based on a few variables that are somewhat subjective and changeable. Are there any changes expected with the cash flow? How much risk is present? How much higher a return must I expect as compensation for the added risk (*risk premium* as discussed in Chapter 6)?

As we change the variables, the answer to what is the value changes, too.

Let me ask this question. If you change the ingredients in a recipe, does it not change the outcome? In other words, if you change the inputs, does it not affect the outputs? Of course, it does. The difference between a muffin recipe and a cake recipe is not much at all.

The process that calculates value is simple arithmetic. Anyone with some simple math skills can calculate value, once they have been shown the formula. If this is true, that anyone can calculate value, then why does everyone calculate different values?

As we have discussed, investors are human beings, and they are charged with emotional responses to changes in their environment. They are greedy. They are fearful. They are afraid to be wrong and they love to be right. These basic truths lead to individual investors coming up with differing valuations. The math is easy, but the variables are subjective and are dependent on the beholder.

One man's treasure is another man's trash, as the saying goes.

If the variables to calculate value are different, the resulting value answer will be different.

For example, Sharon and Dee from our story were asked to calculate the value of a company. They use the same basic formula, but they have to determine the variables themselves.

Dee is more optimistic about the future earnings and risk than Sharon is. Do you think they will arrive at the same intrinsic value? Of course they won't. Different ingredients result in a different cake.

From this, it is easy to see why so many people value companies differently. When people have different opinions about the true value of an asset, you have the makings of a market place where people are willing to buy from those who are willing to sell.

The greater the difference in the opinion of value, the greater swings in the price that it trades for.

If I believed a company to be worth $50 per share based on my mathematics, and you believe it to be worth $100 per share based on your calculations, we have an excellent and logical reason why you would love to buy it for $75 and I would be excited to sell it at the same price.

The reason why stocks rise and fall over time, and in aggregate markets rise and fall, is simply based on this fact. When more people value businesses higher, they are willing to pay more for them and the price goes up (if issued supply remains equal).

On the other hand, when more and more people believe that the companies are worth less, the market price will fall as more people try to sell them (if the available issued supply remains equal).

Crack cocaine and party on the stock market

What does price and value have to do with crack cocaine? They are not really related, unless you are a drug dealer. The reason why I mention it is not because of actual crack cocaine, but because the stock market is sort of a junky at times. Warren Buffet has used the analogy often that the stock market is like a manic depressive person. Both are accurate analogies, although a manic depressive person is not the same as an addict.

The stock market goes through periods of euphoria and crashes, and it is no different than someone who is manic or a junky.

When things are going well, the market follows suit. The party starts, people enjoy themselves and the night progresses. Sometimes the party gets a little out of control and things get crazy. Everyone starts to drink the punch that is spiked with greed and envy. People over indulge to the point of drunkenness. When this is occurring, there is no wrong. There is no end in sight. Logic is put to bed and euphoria rules. Party on dude!

However, the night eventually comes to an end. The party stops, and everyone goes home. The place is a mess and needs to be cleaned up. The drunks are hung over the side of the tub or sprawled out on a bed, suffering from a bad headache and wishing that it would go away. Capitulation is everywhere, with a smell of despondency and sadness in the air. What was in that punch? The longer the party goes on, then the more severe the hangover can be. What seemed like a good idea has its price. Everyone is vowing never to be crazy like that ever again.

Beware, because there is another party not long after and the whole process begins again. Sometimes, it is in the same market as before, but frequently the party just changes houses and cranks the music back up and the drinking begins again.

I use the stock market as the main market for our discussion where this behaviour occurs, but it can happen in any market: bond market, real estate market, foreign exchange market, commodities and even in art and collectibles. They all have their own parties and hangovers. They all have periods of euphoria and periods of bust.

When we look back at some of the bubbles and busts, I am amazed at how we all seem to have perfect hindsight vision. When I first started teaching at the local college, it was the latter part of the 1990's. All the talk was about high tech, e-commerce and the World Wide Web. Nobody wanted to talk about real estate as an investment.

No one wanted to talk about blue chip large companies with stable dividends. Every investor was looking for growth and capital appreciation. There was a tremendous increase in the number of financial advisors entering the profession. Cash was not king; financial assets were.

This junky-like activity drove up prices of almost every company that listed on an exchange. A monkey could literally throw a dart, and whatever he hit was a smashing investment success. This was not because of the monkey or the dart, but it was because everything went up. Investors' demands and expectations were quickly becoming unreasonable.

It was just over thirteen years since the last rockin' party took place in 1987, and everyone swore to never drink the party-punch again. However, they forgot about all that when they heard the music calling them again.

Not long after the talk of Y2K subsided, we had a meltdown. It does not really matter what triggered the end of the party. It never really does. Sometimes, someone calls the cops, and sometimes you just run out of party-punch. The fact is that the party will always come to an end. This time, it happened in and around 2001.

After the party, everyone felt shame. No longer were they going to be so irrational. No longer would they chase returns without the value that they promised.

Financial assets were still popular, but not for the sake of growth and capital appreciation as before. Investors now wanted cash flow. They wanted investments that paid handsome cash flows in the form of dividends. In Canada, we financially engineered a new product called *income trusts*.

This quickly became the darling after the fall. Some investors went in search of cash in other areas such as real estate, and this began another bubble. It resulted in a party less than seven years later when the cops were called in to break up the Collateral Debt party in the USA.

As an investor, it can be unnerving to think that you can get caught up in the euphoria. You, too, could be drinking the party-punch without knowing that it is spiked.

How do you maintain a cool and level head in the middle of all this? How do you keep from getting caught up in all the irrational exuberance that parties seem to invite us to? How do you maintain the principle that you get value for the price you pay? The answer, which I have already stated, is simple in theory but very difficult in practice: *intellectual framework*.

By sticking to your intellectual framework, you will reduce the chances of overpaying for your investments. By following your strategic allocation, it will help to ensure that you do not get caught in a specific market bubble. By executing on dynamic allocation, you will effectively and systematically be "selling high and buying low".

By determining the intrinsic value as the means to determine price, it will keep you on the good side of the ledger.

In the next chapter, we are going to further the discussion about value and price. However, we will not focus on investment assets but instead on investment management performance. Are you price-driven or value-driven?

CHAPTER 10 ~ BOTULISM, SALMONELLA AND E. COLI

Mitch and Meg's story

"New apartment/ new beginnings," Mitch Belman thought to himself as he headed home from work on a beautiful Friday afternoon in July. Today was the first night in their new apartment together. They had delivered all their belongings, which did not amount to much, that morning before heading to work.

The workday went by quickly, as Mitch had spent most of his day dreaming about the new life that he and his fiancée Meg were embarking on. They had been together for a few years, but with the anticipation of their upcoming marriage next year, they decided to live together to help reduce costs associated with living separately. The money they saved would be used to pay for the wedding. As they hoped not to use it all, it would also provide a down payment on a new house for them. It would also be a home for their cat named Bean, a hamster named Allen and the fish that is aptly named: Fish, of course.

Mitch was heading west on the highway, and the sun glared into the cab of the van and directly into his eyes. He could hardly see the road ahead. The crest of the big hill he was on tilted the van toward the sky and directly into the sun ahead. Mitch decided to pull over for a coffee and text his fiancee about their first supper together.

Meg Billmer worked only a few minutes from their new apartment. She will be able to walk to work, which she will enjoy. It meant that she could frequently go home at lunch to take care of her "kiddies": Bean, Allen and Fish, of course. Meg decided that she would stay for a little longer at work to finish some things on her desk. It wasn't to impress her employer, but she was just that type of worker. She was the type that arrives early and leaves late. Besides, Mitch would not be back for another hour, she thought.

As she continued working, Meg's cell phone suddenly buzzed and made her jump in her seat. It was Mitch.

Mitch: *"Hey baby!* ☺*"* It was typical Mitch, Meg thought to herself.

Meg: *"Baby?! What's up?"*

Mitch: *"Not much. You? Supper tonight?"*

Meg: *"No texting and driving! Supper- haven't thought about it"*

Mitch: *"Not texting/driving! Supper? Pick something up?"*

Meg thought about the cost, but she also thought that it would be nice to go out and celebrate. Besides, there was no food in the apartment yet, and their dishes were still packed in the boxes.

Meg: *"How about going out? Hamburgers and fries? At Gourmet Burger?"*

Mitch: *"Sure. Hamburgers, side of fries and your loving eyes!! Yummie.* ☺ *Do the unpacking after"*

Mitch considered the idea. He and Meg loved Gourmet Burger. Who wouldn't, as it was the classiest burger joint in the whole town? Like Meg, Mitch considered whether they should save the money instead. Both Meg and Mitch liked a simple, uncomplicated life.

They cherished simple things, and they relaxed easily into the world around them without the need of luxuries. This was a common thread that tied them together so well.

> Mitch: *"Or can I pick up some groceries and I cook for you? Mitch's Special Burgers!! LOL"*

Mitch was certainly not a cook: Special Burgers indeed! No amount of money saved would be worth the torment of food poisoning. The basic image of Mitch working in a kitchen made her giggle and squirm at the same time. Toast slightly blackened with a side of cold canned beans was his specialty. Meg understood that he felt the same about spending the extra money at the Gourmet Burger Shop.

> Meg: *"Thanks for offer sweet-thing! I want to live to attend our wedding, Mitchie ☺ LOL! How about Burger Palace? Cheap but good."*

Mitch was so relieved. He had no clue how to make a hamburger patty, let alone how to cook it. It was a brave offer, but the experience was full of potential failure. Burger Palace was not the same as the incredible Gourmet Burger. It was a simple place with good burgers, relaxed atmosphere and, most importantly, no one would die.

> Mitch: *"Sweet-thing?! Yeah, better safe than sorry. Burger Palace, it is! Yum?! Haha!"*

> Meg: *"Meet you there in an hour?"*

> Mitch: *"Awesome. Love you baby!"*

> Meg: "Baby?!!! Love you too!

Mitch put the truck back in gear and continued on his way with a big smile. *New life/new beginnings* would begin safely at the discount Burger Palace.

How often in life do we have the same question put to us? I would argue that it happens daily, sometimes several times a day. We might not see it. Something needs to be done and we have a choice, as all of life is about choices. We can do it entirely ourselves, we can let someone else do the "heavy lifting" and we can do the rest, or we can let someone else do everything for us.

Many people have a view that to pay someone to do something you can easily do yourself is a waste of money. That is not how I was raised. You were probably raised to think the same way. We view it as an act of laziness to allow someone else to do something that we can perfectly do ourselves.

Sometimes that is the case, and sometimes it is not so. This chapter is a discussion about money, service, experience and value. It is primarily about price and value. We will be looking at the cost of something as compared to the value of something.

The relationship between price and value resonates throughout many things in life. It is true not only in personal finance but in many other areas as well. The main question always comes down to this: "Am I getting fair value for what I am paying?"

In the last chapter, we talked about price and value from the point of view of investments. Specifically, we discussed the value of a business vs the price for the business. We went over the intrinsic value and how price is rarely equal to intrinsic value.

It is true about many things when you think about it. What am I paying, and what am I getting for my money? The problem that arises is that the value is hard to pinpoint when it is based on variables like performance and experience.

Let me expand on Mitch and Meg's story. They are a cute couple who are just starting out on their life's journey together. Mitch is heading home and he charmingly asks Meg what she wants for supper. He offers to either go out or to cook for her. Meg chooses not to die from either botulism or salmonella. She would prefer to see her wedding day. What are the choices that this couple has to make, and what value are they going to get for the money that they will spend?

I am sure that Mitch and Meg's decision is something that you have had to make in the past. Do we cook the meal ourselves, pick up part of the meal and cook the rest or do we simply go out and let a restaurant do the work? I will come back to this in a moment.

Hamburger logic

In our local area, similar to your own, we have several restaurant choices—especially for hamburgers. We have your typical fast-food outlets that pump out the burgers in advance and have them wrapped under the usual red glow of a heat lamp. We will call this the Discount Burger store.

We also have other burger places that will cook the burger on demand, like the Burger Palace in the story. They will customize the burger so that you can have it "your way", and they proceed to wrap it in a foil wrapper. This is a slightly better burger. Lastly, we have a place like Gourmet Burger in the story. The product is customized to your liking, it is bigger and better, and it is served on a real plate with steel cutlery.

Discount Burger produces a thin burger on a plain bun, maybe a sesame seed, and it comes pre-ordained with ketchup, lettuce, pickles, onions and maybe a processed cheese slice. The side is generally a bag of heavily salted shoe-string fries. The experience consists of standing in line, being served as a number, getting your own soft drink at the communal fountain and sitting on hard plastic chairs that are attached to a cafeteria-style table setting. Plastic forks and knives are available, but they are never really used. The burger fits easily in one hand and the fries are made for finger picking. The cost for the meal, for the sake of argument, is $5.

Burger Palace is a slight step up from Discount Burger. It produces a larger patty with the toppings of your choice (including some more exotic choices from the normal toppings), on a bun of more character and with a side order of onion rings or thick-cut fries. The experience, although much like Discount Burger, is slightly improved. You stand in line to make your order, it is served on a plastic tray with plastic cutlery, but the ambiance in the dining area is more comfortable. The seats have a plush surface, although they are still hard because of the plastic below. The chairs are not attached to the tables or fixed to the floors. The cost for the meal, for the sake of our discussion, is $8.

The third choice of going out for a burger and fries is The Gourmet Burger. This is not the real name of any particular place that I know of, but it represents the many local places that have an upscale burger offering. The burger it produces is chef-made from quality meat. The names and selection of the burgers are inspired, intriguing and exotic.

They are topped with fresh ingredients that you might not have at home. Instead of just chopped onions, you can have caramelized onions, and instead of plain ketchup they offer dozens of sauce variations. There is not a processed cheese slice in the house, and the list of other condiments fills a whole page. The sides are as daunting as the condiments: spiced wedge fries, sweet potato fries and dip, soups, salads, jumbo onion rings, calamari and even shrimp skewers. There are no line-ups.

There is only a smiling server, a comfortable table and chairs or a private booth with real linen and silverware. No waxed paper cups of soda with a straw sticking out of spill-proof lid taken from a self-serve fountain, but rather you have a choice of beer, wine or other beverages. The cost of this is around $20 per plate.

How much do you think it would cost you to make a burger at home? Well, it might cost you a few dollars per burger at most.

My first question to you is this: why would someone like you pay $5 at Discount Burger, $10 at Burger Palace or even $20 at Gourmet Burger when you can make it cheaper at home? The second question is: why would someone pay upwards of $20 for a burger when they can get it for $5 or $10?

The first answer is pretty simple, and it comes down to three basic reasons: a) you can't cook, and the only option is to outsource the activity, b) you don't have time to cook a burber or the time to learn how to cook one, or c) you don't have the desire to cook and you would rather be doing something else.

If you can't cook a burger, you are not alone. There are many men and women who simply do not know how to cook anything, let alone a hamburger. Beef needs to achieve around 140°F to ensure that the nasty stuff is dead. An uncooked or undercooked burger patty can kill you. Although this is unlikely, the bacteria that you may be ingesting from uncooked beef (Salmonella, E Coli, Listeria and Campylobacter) will give you severe cramping and bloody diarrhea for 5 to 7 days. Nobody wants that. Meg wants to make it to her wedding day! That is a solid reason why you may want to outsource the activity of burger cooking.

The second reason is that there is simply not enough time to either cook a burger or to learn how to cook one. Life is busy. Certain fast food chains cater to this reality in our society, and over the last 50 or 60 years, they have become dominant food providers. The Drive-Thru is testament to how busy we have become. Joseph and his pregnant wife Mary did not pull into the Trot-Thru on their journey to Bethlehem to grab a quick burger for the road. How many times have you been so busy that you needed to get a quick bite to eat? Again, time as a commodity is not always available.

The last reason is that we really have no desire to cook or to learn how to cook. I might really love burgers, but I would much rather be writing this book than standing on my deck and grilling a burger right now on the BBQ. It may also be the case where you can't cook simply because you just don't care to learn. You might prefer to spend the time learning some other skill besides cooking.

All of these reasons are logical conclusions as to why someone would prefer to pay a few dollars more to have it done for them.

My second question was: why would someone like you be willing to pay a higher cost for a hamburger at one location versus another? Why would someone pay $20 for a burger plate instead of $5 or $10? Well, are they paying extra for the burger or are they paying for something more than just the burger? Sure, the quality of the hamburger and the condiments are better and they demand a higher cost, but does that still justify 3 or 4 times the price over Discount Burger or double the price of Burger Palace? From a functional point of view of eating to survive, the calorie intake would be not much greater than the other offerings. So, why pay more?

It all comes down to the *experience*. The value that comes from the actual product is not just in the burger itself. The taste is likely to be much better, but the real value comes from the *experience* of having that meal. What would be the difference between enjoying the meal in the gourmet location and taking the same burger into a dark room with no furniture? Imagine closing off all your senses except smell and taste. I would argue that the experience would be far less enjoyable. Smell and taste are important, but so are the other variables that contribute to our experience. This is no different than reading a romance novel in a crowded city bus compared to enjoying it on a quiet tropical beach. Great experiences magnify the end result.

We would pay more because the likelihood of getting a quality burger with a terrific experience is far greater and the chance of success is almost guaranteed.

Let us now look at how the hamburger analogy relates to your personal finance and wealth creation.

Results or price?

Are you a results-driven or price-driven investor? Do you care more about lowering your cost or obtaining your financial goals?

Immediately, most people will say that they want to reach their goals, but they will pepper this statement with "*but*".

- *but* I don't want to waste money
- *but* the cost reduces my return and the ability to reach my goal
- *but* why pay someone if I can do it myself
- *but* you can't just ignore cost.

So, let us just agree to one statement before we go further-*we are all results driven* and *we all care about cost*. I am not here to say that you should ignore cost or that cost is not a contributor to net returns. Only a fool would ignore costs. As a matter of fact, in the absence of value, the price of anything is truly irrelevant. This is no different than knowing the fact that one baseball team scored 5 runs while not knowing the runs that the other team scored!

The above statements are misleading because they do not address the issue of value. If we re-phrase the "buts", they become results-driven questions about the price or costs:

- *but* what is the value I am getting for the cost?
- *but* what value do I get in reaching my goal in exchange for this cost to reach my goal?
- *but* what value do I get if I pay someone?

- *but* you can't just ignore value!

A few years ago, I replaced the deck on the back of my house. It was a pretty big job, and it took a few weeks to complete. Destruction of the old deck, removal of the waste wood, new supporting structures, frame, decking, railing and painting—all of it had to be dealt with.

I had a choice to make about this, and it came down to three things:

a) Do I want to replace the deck myself?
b) Do I want to outsource certain jobs and do the rest myself?
c) Do I want to outsource the whole job to a professional?

I chose the second. I removed the old structure and decided to paint. Knowing we wanted to put a hot tub on the deck, it was clear that I would prefer to get a professional to do the under structure to support the weight of the incoming hot tub. The carpenter also did the rest of the construction as well.

I could spend the time learning how to build the deck. I did not have the time to replace it myself. More importantly, I did not have the desire either.

The rest of the work was also outsourced, because I did not have time to finish the job before my deadline. Besides, the professionals ended up doing a fantastic job compared to the deck that I would finished. The cost to outsource to the carpenter was substantial if we only look at the cost. In the absence of value, EVERYTHING is expensive.

I could tell you any amount that I paid him, and that amount would seem ridiculous without knowing what he did or seeing the end result. In my mind, it was money well spent, and I am actually sitting on this deck right now as I write this chapter.

Putting our personal financial decisions into action is the same:

- we can do all of it,

- we can do some of it, or
- we can do none of it.

To be quite honest, in order to be well on your way to understanding the world of personal finance, to the point where you can do everything yourself (at least virtually everything), it only takes three things: time, desire and an average amount of intelligence. If you have these three things, you could do virtually everything on your own. I have yet to see anyone truly do anything but mediocre at best with this approach. This is not because of lack of intelligence, as the vast majority of people possess this quality. I will share with you two of the reasons why DIY personal finance is simply going to fail in the long term and, therefore, is a waste of your time.

First of all, your *willpower* to do the job will be on a dwindling desire. You might have all the energy and desire on a Sunday night after the football game to review your accounts or on a Tuesday as an excuse to get out of cutting the grass. The problem arises when you do not have the same desire but you NEED to handle something that is timely. What you once thought was easy or enjoyable quickly becomes a job, and things tend to go unchecked or become underserved. There are other demands in your life, and they will require your time and reduce your desire. I only need to point to the pile of paper on many people's filing cabinets that is waiting for a rainy day to come (which the weatherman says has already passed).

Secondly, logic and emotion are huge factors in this area. Do you know that most barbers go to other barbers to get their own hair cut? Go ahead and say, "Obviously." Most dentists do not pull their own teeth. Go ahead and say, "Duh, no doubt!" Well, financial advisors will often seek the opinion of other financial advisors! Strange maybe, but it is true nonetheless.

Think about this for a minute. A barber and a dentist go to another barber and dentist because they can't see what is going on behind their own head or inside their own mouth. The barber does not go to the dentist for a haircut, and the dentist surely does not go to the barber for tooth extractions. This would be ludicrous. The financial advisor, no matter how much schooling he or she has, will always fight the battle between logic and emotion when making decisions. We are all human. It is because advisors themselves often have difficulty in rationalizing their ideas because of the emotional tie to their money, fear and greed. If you read my acknowledgements, you will see the names of many people who are my trusted advisors. They are my sounding board.

Now, with that said, you can try to do everything yourself. It will likely fail, or it may achieve mediocrity at best over the long term. That is the best case scenario.

Doing everything yourself will lower your cost substantially, and it would be the wisest choice if value was not a consideration.

Wait, Jeff! What about all those personal finance books, magazines and newspaper columns that say you CAN do it yourself. Are they lying to us? Well, I am going to say it: yes! In a strange twist to the DIY investor approach, they are simply suggesting that you use *them* as the advisor. By buying the money magazine or the yearly book on investing, they can lead you to profits at reduced costs. Hogwash! The magazine is acting as an advisor--a very low-cost, low-accountability advisor--but an advisor regardless.

The second way to manage our finances is to outsource what we don't know how to do. This is, by far, the most popular choice. We can appreciate that we simply do not have the knowledge to do some of the jobs properly. We can also appreciate that we do not have the time to learn what financial professionals spend years to learn in certain areas.

We can reach deep into our hearts to find that we might not have the desire to take on the task of learning about certain fields in personal finance. Maybe mortgages interest you, and you love to learn about those, but you can't stand reading about insurance. Maybe taxes are your thing, but the idea of making investment decisions makes you nauseous.

This approach is popular, because personal finance involves many areas and some are easy to tackle yourself. For example, many people happily hire an investment counsellor, but they can manage the day-to-day banking and cash flow needs themselves.

You could also outsource some of the financial grunt work, while handling the stuff that you are capable of by yourself. This, of course, would reduce cost and/or concentrate the costs on the areas that you most need to outsource.

Understand that, in this approach, it very often ensures that the individual makes the financial decision. However, he hires a professional to consistently put forward ideas and recommendations to increase the chance of success over the long run.

The last approach is to outsource everything. This is very uncommon and is limited to very special situations. This could be where a person is incapacitated from handling their own affairs due to mental health, physical health or some other constraint.

Do you need a financial advisor or wealth manager?

The decision for the individual is simply this: *What do I need to outsource, and to whom?*

Do I outsource all, some or none?

My wife and I got together just before I finished school and began my career as a wealth advisor. Of course, while sitting around with family, the question would inevitably come up about my career choice and what the job was about. My mother-in-law, who I like very much (in case she reads this), once commented to me: "A financial advisor? They are mostly for the rich people. You have to have lots of money to need a financial advisor." She was part joking and part serious. I found this comment to be fascinating! I replied, being part joking and part serious, "I guess only healthy people should see their doctors then!"

She had a great question, and it is one that often gets dismissed because of the cost/value discussion. It gets dismissed FAR too often because of cost. This is what stands out to individuals and what the media attention talks about far more than results. The financial planning industry has made a tremendous mistake in the past by communicating the results that clients experience, mainly because they are always on the defensive about cost. The value, my friends, outweighs the so-called costs more often than not.

Choosing your wealth advisor

So now you are set to explore the possibility of working with a trusted advisor or to review the current advisor that you have already.

Before we get into that list, we must first understand that not all advisors are equal in capabilities and strengths. In my opinion, approximately 99% of advisors are quality people who are doing an admirable job for their clients. There is the 1% of the group that are questionable in their behaviour and approach with clients—but this is very, very rare and is no different than any other industry or sector. Look at the people that you work with in your career. Do you know of anyone in your own professional line of work who was questionable with respect to their capacity or their conduct?

When I say "not all advisors are equal", I mean that some may be a better fit than others for you and your family.

Where should you start? Well, the first place I recommend people look to is within their circle of family and friends. You might know some people in your life that you feel have a certain financial acumen. Ask these people for referrals. You might also look at various financial association websites. These sites generally offer a search tool for certain types of advisors in your area.

Make a list of two or three of them and give them a call. Make an appointment, and meet with them face-to-face. I assure you that a quality advisor will not mind you coming in to see if they are the best fit for you. As a matter of fact, most quality advisors offer the first meeting without charge, not only so you can see if you want to work with them, but so they can also determine if they *want* to work with you.

Some advisors will take anyone. Quality advisors demand that you fit the type of client they are willing to take on. This does not always have to do with how wealthy you are. Why is this? Well, they realize that the relationship between an advisor and a client is a long-term relationship based on trust and an ability to work together.

Quality advisors will screen you in the first meeting as much as you are screening them. This is fair and it should be expected. They have built a business on trust and professionalism. Quality advisors will only be willing to work with you if they believe that they can be of value to you and are able to maintain a strong relationship over time. In our office, my willingness to take on a client is based on three basic criteria, and I would expect most quality advisors you talk to would have the same:

1. you fully disclose all information that will allow me to do my job,
2. you agree with our team philosophy about building wealth, and
3. we truly believe that we can add significant value to your financial lives.

The decision to take on a client is not actually based on how much our office will benefit from having a particular client. The relationship is the most important factor, as we will always be compensated appropriately if we do the right job. Quality advisors know that fair compensation takes care of itself when you work hard for your clients.

Ok, so now you will have made a list of potential Advisors, and some appointments are made. What should you look for when interviewing the advisor? The whole process is very much like a job interview. The Advisor wants to know if they want to work for you, and you want to determine if this is the person you want to hire.

Let's see if we can narrow down how to choose the best advisor for your family. I have put together a list of different things that investors should look for when searching out the best advisor for your family.

These are the criteria that you should examine:

Credentials

The easiest criteria to look for and find is the formal education that the advisor has. The credentials will most often show up on their website, business card or anywhere their name is prominently displayed. If you cannot find their credentials, just simply ask them. Common credentials you will find are: CFP (Certified Financial Planner), RFP (Registered Financial Planner), CIM (Canadian Investment Manager), CLU (Chartered Life Underwriter), TEP (Trust and Estate Practitioner, FMA (Financial Management Advisor) and

PFP (Personal Financial Planner).

Experience

Formal education is one thing. Experience, or informal education, is another. The number of years as an active advisor can make a big difference in offering that stable and confident approach. Advisors who have been around for 15 or 20+ years have seen one or two business cycles, several market drops and rebounds, and they have seen clients move through the different stages of the Personal Financial Lifecycle. This is not just knowledge. When *experience* is partnered with *education,* the result is wisdom. There is a caveat to some investors who wish to work with advisors that have been around a while.

An advisor who has decades of experience may have time thresholds that are expensive and limited. For investors who are just starting out, the best advisors are those who are also just starting out as well. They have the time to work with each client and the cost to hire these advisors is far less. If you are looking to work with an advisor who is relatively new, ask if they have a mentor that is available to help with clients. Often, this will be the case, and that leverage is of great value to you.

Peer Group Associations

To be an advisor of quality means spending time and money to build up the value that we bring to clients and to the marketplace. A quality advisor knows that they must continually upgrade and strive for more knowledge, which comes from study on their own and with other advisors. The financial world is a dynamic place where basic truths remain, but laws, products, and markets change every day. To stay abreast of this change requires both time and effort. If an advisor is not willing to put in this time and effort, you should walk away from them. A simple test to determine their commitment to the industry is to ask what associations or industry groups they belong to.

Specializations

Advisors may offer some form of specialization in a specific area, such as: credit counselling, tax, investment, insurance, estates or money coaching. This is important if you are an investor who has decided to do some activities yourself and then outsource some other financial activities. The designations, although not a perfect way to sift through skill sets, can be a great beginning spot to see which areas that advisors are stronger in.

Fee structure

There are three basic fee structures that clients must be aware of: fee for service, commission and a combination of the two. This becomes important when you are trying to determine the value of their advice. You may be looking only to pay a fee in order to get the advice for certain areas, but eventually you will have to implement the strategy, and that may be for a service that earns a commission. Sometimes you might not have the available capital to pay a fee-for-service advisor, and a commission-based approach might be more advantageous.

There are benefits and pitfalls to both of the first two structures, and it is important that the investor determines for themselves the best approach. The last structure is very rare, as there is an inherent conflict between recommending a financial product and then also getting paid a commission on its purchase. Investors would do well to understand the reason behind a fee and commission structure with an advisor.

After creating a short list of potential advisors and having met with a few of them, you will have a very short list of two or maybe three that are potentials. The next step is the biggest one. Which one do you trust with your gut and would be the best fit for you? Put education, fee structure, experience, credentials, specializations and peer group associations aside now (as these are what brought them down to maybe two possible advisors).

It is time to reach down inside and determine which of them that you are most comfortable with and that you trust the most. At this point, the answer should be pretty clear.

To close out this chapter, let us just review the basic ideas:

1. You have a very important financial choice between doing it yourself or not.

2. If you choose to use an advisor, which I recommend, it is important to quantify both value and cost

3. Choosing a quality advisor can be done by

    - asking friends for referrals,
    - interviewing them, and
    - determining who best fits your needs and is the most trustworthy.

SUMMARY

YOUR story

All of the chapters in this book were written with one mission in mind: to bring back the common sense and fundamental truths about money, investing and financial freedom—for YOUR benefit. I wanted to share with you that reaching your financial goals in a world that has become overly complex can still be accomplished. To do this, I wanted to show you the tools that keep simplicity at the core of the decision making process and help you to stay focused on your wealth.

The book has covered many topics over ten chapters. Let me summarize the main concepts and how you can use them in a meaningful way to regain control of your personal finances and investments. If nothing else, it will become an excellent starting point as you continue to work with your experienced and trusted wealth advisor.

Concept #1: You are going to die!

We are on this earth for a short time. We are born and we die. We have three basic periods in our life from which we can plan: Learn, Earn, and Yearn.

Action #1: Draw a horizontal line that is broken into three equal parts by two vertical lines. At the left side of the horizontal line, write your date of birth. On the right side of the horizontal line write the year of your death (i.e. add 80 years from your date of birth. If you think you will die sooner or live longer, then use a different number). Next, above each of the three sections, from left to right, print the words: Learn, Earn, and Yearn.

Now, here comes the hard part that requires thinking and a little bit of dreaming. Write at the end of each of the three sections the approximate ages that these events will occur or did occur. The year that you finished formal education goes at the end of Learn. The day you finished working full-time and headed into retirement goes at the end of Earn. Once this is done, start to fill in the more micro life highlights that happened or you wish to happen in your life between date of birth and date of death. Write down the dates that you: got married, had children, paid off the mortgage, bought a cottage, attended your child's wedding, went on an exotic holiday or had great-grandchildren. Dream a little! If you are married, it is a good idea to do this together, as you are sharing a life together.

Action #2: Discuss with an older or even a younger family member in order to discover how the Learn, Earn and Yearn years have changed between them and you.

These two action items will give you a graphic image and a personal experience to solidify our core financial principles. Hopefully, this will resonate in your mind and put into perspective the need to plan ahead for your financial freedom.

Concept #2: Man at Work vs Money at Work

Financial security is not measured solely based on age, education, job, debt or the level of assets. Financial security is achieved at the inflection point when Man-at-Work can be converted to Money-at-Work. Man-at-Work is an activity that not only sustains a family through the earning years but is used to build up capital for future money-at-work during the yearning years.

Action #1: On a piece of paper, write down how much you spend for the basic essentials of life currently. Basic essentials are shelter, food, clothing and transportation. Once you record this amount, determine if there are any things in these categories that will change on the date you go from *earning* to *yearning*. Now, adjust the number you had based on these changes. This is your essentials amount.

Now, add what you believe to be the annual amount that you will require to maintain the lifestyle that you want. These lifestyle items could include annual spending on travel, a second car, a boat or cottage. The list is up to you. Once you have the annual amounts for each (essentials and lifestyle), you have the basic requirement that you have to achieve for the *yearning* years. Subtract from this any annual pension income you may be entitled to. This is the net amount that you need to achieve, and you should now multiply this by twenty (to cover at least 20 years of retirement).

This number, although it may seem large, is your simplified Money-at-Work goal. In the simplest terms, this is the amount of money that you need to have in personal savings in order to reach your point of financial security in retirement.

Concept #3: Pay Yourself First

Now that we have determined your required Money-at-Work goal, which will provide us with our much desired financial security, we must layout the game plan for achieving the goal.

The Man-at-Work income has two purposes: it sustains us to live in the present and it provides an amount of savings for the future. The wise man knows that a portion of what Man-at-Work earns must be used to build for the future.

Action #1: Prepare a list of all the items that you spend money on each month. Do not include the amounts, but rather just write the description of the item for now. When you have written the three top items, stop what you are doing. Go back and make sure that the number one item is *Pay Yourself First*. It does not matter at this point how much it is or where it goes, it is just important to realize that a certain amount of money is needed right at the top of the list to pay for your future.

Once you have listed all the items, then fill in the amounts, starting with essentials (which now includes "PYF- Pay Yourself First"). This essential list includes: PYF, shelter, food, clothing and basic transportation. Before you write down any other amounts, write down an amount equal to 7% of your take-home pay. If you take home $4,000 every month, then write down $280 to pay yourself first. If you have never saved for yourself, this amount will look painful to accomplish. All of the remaining amounts will get filled in only after this one is done. Once complete, make sure that the amount going out each month is equal to amount coming in each month. If it is not, adjust the non-essential spending items in order to make the numbers balance. You cannot adjust the essentials items.

Once this exercise is complete, you will find one of two things occurred: a) you already save enough in the PYF and we can move on to the next exercise, or b) you feel very uncomfortable with the PYF amount and are trying to rationalize some of the non-essential items that you _want_ to call essential (but they are not!)

The exercise is meant to place the onus on you for your own future. Imagine that you are responsible for yourself. If you fail to achieve financial security, this will be the point in time that you can come back to that could have changed everything. It is truly a game-changer between successful "future-you" and mediocre "future-you".

Concept #4: Your Personal Wealth Management Strategy

This concept is to help build a screen from the clutter of everyday news. Most of the time, the news that we read does not apply to us, and we need to cut through all the babble and rhetoric. The best way to do this is to have a target or goal in mind. When we set specific targets or goals, we can aim and concentrate on those things and ignore the noise around us.

Action #1: Grab a newspaper and head to the financial or money section. Choose an article that is written by a journalist. With two different-colored highlighters, stroke each sentence as either being statistic or opinion–one colour for each. At the end of the exercise, compare the number of sentences that do not contain either. Try it again with another article.

Action #2: Take inventory of what you *owe* and what you *own*. On a piece of paper, create two columns, one on each side. Title the column on the left side *"Assets (what I own)"*. On the right column, title it *"Liabilities (what I owe)"*. Under the assets list, write the value of all of the things that you own with a short description for each. On the right side, under the liabilities list, write down all of the amounts of the debts that you have with a short description for each. Subtract the liabilities from the assets. This is your net worth.

Action #3. On a piece of paper, write down the title "Short Term Goals". Get two other pieces of paper and write on each of the titles "Medium Term Goals" and "Long Term Goals". These are your three planning areas.

After you have titled the three pages as described, then write down 1 to 3 goals for each of the three planning areas. Be very specific about the goal that you want to achieve in each of the planning areas. The goal should state: *what* it is, *when* you must achieve it and how you must achieve it. For example, if you want to save for a house, then state the type of house (size, type and cost), when you would like to achieve it (specific date) and how you are going to achieve it (monthly savings, inheritance or sell something of value).

You now have produced a basic inventory of where you are today (net worth) and where you want to get to (goals). Compare your goals on the sheets and refer back to the newspaper. See if anything in the financial or money columns helps to move you towards your goals, and ignore them if they just create a bunch of noise. You must avoid topics that confuse rather than help. The information may even move you further away from reaching your goals.

Concept #5: IPS and Your Asset Allocation Method

Capital markets have historically supported, with empirical evidence, that stocks outperform bonds and bonds outperform cash. Ownership achieves greater returns than "loanership". By allocating our wealth among the various asset classes (using prudent diversification), we can target our return and level of risk in order to match these investments with our unique circumstances, needs and objectives.

Action point: Take your net worth statement that you just completed, divide up your current wealth and see how it is allocated. Divide the assets into two basic groups: growth (ownership) and income/safety (loanership). Calculate the percentage that you have in each area.

Now, for the sake of simplifying the exercise and to help further the concept of asset allocation, subtract your current age from 100. Compare the percentages that you have in these areas with the amount you currently should have based on age. For example, based on this simple rule of thumb, a 40-year-old person should have 60% in growth assets and 40% invested in income and safety assets.

You can now make some adjustments to what you feel is a more appropriate allocation for your situation. This is based on your own objective, risk tolerance, time horizon, required return- and any other special needs. For example, a higher risk tolerance may mean that there is more appetite for growth assets, and it could justify having 75% in growth assets or more. If your objective is safety of capital or you have a short time horizon until you need the money, the allocation to growth may need to be reduced significantly.

Discuss this exercise with your quality wealth advisor, or have it ready when you interview a potential new advisor that you meet with. It is a great tool to get a feel for how they think about investment management.

Concept #6: Price vs Value

Are you getting value for what you are paying? Are you paying for a Gourmet Burger but receiving a Burger Palace entrée?

You have a choice–a very important choice when it comes to your financial wellbeing. You can choose to take on the whole wealth management role yourself and make all the decisions without ANY outside help. You can also choose to assume some tasks that you are capable of performing and willing to do while outsourcing other activities that may be too time-consuming or difficult. Lastly, you can outsource the whole wealth management job to someone, allowing them to guide you to financial security. The choice is up to you, and it is a choice that you MUST make. If you don't, your outcome will ultimately never reach any particular goal because you had not taken any action.

Action point: Spend some time reviewing the costs associated with your current situation and the current source of advice that you are following. Learn about fees, whether they are hidden or not. Summarize the fees that you pay for asset management, banking services, insurance, tax preparation and general financial advisor fees.

Ask yourself if these fees are warranted for the service that you are getting. Understand that professionals need to be paid, as no one works for free; however, the price you pay should line up with the value that they are providing you and your family.

SUMMARY

Concept #7: Choosing a Quality Wealth Advisor

There are literally thousands of financial planners and financial advisors across Canada. Once you decide to hire an advisor (which the vast majority of people should), how can you know which one is the quality wealth advisor that is right for your family? If you already have an advisor, how can you tell if they are a quality wealth advisor?

Action #1: Determine which of the financial services that you would like to outsource, i.e. ones that you cannot take care of yourself properly or do not have adequate time to commit to. Make a list of each of these activities on the left-side margin of a piece of paper. For example: tax preparation, tax advice, insurances, goal setting, planning, budgeting, portfolio management, estate planning, debt repayment, education funding and any others that you can think of.

Action #2: Speak to friends, family and co-workers in order to get some names of advisors that they currently work with. You may also look on industry websites or do an internet search to come up with some names. Once you have the names, check out their professional website, or call their office to ask questions about the services they provide to clients and any areas of specialization. Write the names of the advisors who would best serve your list of needs.

For example, if you want someone who covers all of the above mentioned categories well, you might first want someone who is designated as a Certified Financial Planner.

Action #3: Out of the list of names that qualify as potential quality advisors, book an appointment with two or three of them to discuss your situation and to get to know their personalities.

YOUR NEXT STEP

Now, it is time to take the next step in your financial adventure.

First, I truly hope that you have enjoyed this book, and more importantly, that the book has helped you to regain control of your financial life. My intention has been to offer you a simplified view of basic financial concepts, ones that most individuals must deal with in order to reach their financial goals.

I wrote this book, not to try to answer all of your questions, but rather to help you to develop a base from which you can ask the questions that you need to have answered. I encourage you to read more about personal finance and educate yourself as much as possible, so that you can make intelligent decisions about your financial future.

I am here for YOU. Nothing would make me happier than to be able to personally lead you through the waters to your desired money goals.

If you are ready to finally take control of your financial future and achieve the security that you desire, then the NEXT STEP is in your hands.

Take a moment and contact me right now, using the contact details below, so that we can determine the best way forward for you and your family:

> **Phone (Ontario, Canada):** 613-253-8934
>
> **Fill out an online request:** www.JeffKeill.com
>
> **Visit our office**: Keill & Associates, 81 Bridge Street, Carleton Place, ON, K7C 2V4, Canada

My staff and I are waiting for your call or support request.

I sincerely wish you all the best for your financial future.

Jeffery A Keill

Jeffery A Keill CFP CIM FMA

Senior Wealth Advisor

Keill & Associates

ABOUT THE AUTHOR

Since 1992, Jeff has worked as a wealth manager, helping busy families to set and achieve their financial goals. He has aligned himself with a highly-motivated and client-centric team of professionals. Together, they strive to provide family-focused wealth management solutions so families may "live their dream" while being free of financial worry.

Jeff has been a respected professor for the School of Business and School of Part Time Studies at a local college, as well as being an active board member for the college's Financial Services program.

As a public speaker, Jeff has delivered his message of financial hope to many organizations, both in the public and private sectors. Jeff resides just outside of Carleton Place, Ontario, Canada, with his wife Teresa.

ABOUT THE PUBLISHER

WRITE your book.
BUILD your brand.
CREATE your platform.
BROADCAST your message.
EXPAND your reach and income...

Perissos Media helps business owners, speakers, consultants, professionals, sales teams, ministry leaders and inspired individuals to PUBLISH books, audio and video training products and other marketing materials.

Our goal is to BUILD your platform and ELEVATE you to "expert status" in your field—with all the financial and lifestyle benefits that come with it.

We start with dialogue and planning, and then we organize recorded interviews, transcription, editing, formatting, cover design, branding and numerous marketing strategies.

What we produce is a PLATFORM for influential people to expand their reach thorough books and workbooks, audio and video training packages, speaking engagements and a global PRESENCE on Amazon, Google, social media and beyond.

For a FREE copy of one of our Amazon books to help you to publish your message to a greater audience, please visit:

www.IWantToPublish.com

We look forward to serving you,

Jerry Kuzma

Director, PerissosGroup.com

www.ingramcontent.com/pod-product-compliance
Lightning Source LLC
Chambersburg PA
CBHW071428180526
45170CB00001B/257